SLOW COOKER

A CELEBRATION OF
THE SLOW COOKER

SLOW COOKER

A CELEBRATION OF THE SLOW COOKER

This edition published by Parragon Books Ltd in 2016
LOVE FOOD is an imprint of Parragon Books Ltd

Parragon Books Ltd
Chartist House
15–17 Trim Street
Bath BA1 1HA, UK
www.parragon.com/lovefood

ISBN 978-1-4748-5395-8

Printed in China

New photography by Mike Cooper
New recipes by Robin Donovan
Introductions by Sarah Bush

Notes for the Reader
This book uses both metric and imperial measurements. Follow the same units of measurement throughout; do not mix metric and imperial. All spoon measurements are level: teaspoons are assumed to be 5 ml, and tablespoons are assumed to be 15 ml. Unless otherwise stated, milk is assumed to be full fat, eggs and individual fruits and vegetables are medium, pepper is freshly ground black pepper and salt is table salt. A pinch of salt is calculated as 1/16 of a teaspoon. Unless otherwise stated, all root vegetables should be peeled prior to using.

The times given are an approximate guide only. Preparation times differ according to the techniques used by different people and the cooking times may also vary from those given.

For best results, use a food thermometer when cooking meat. Check the latest government guidelines for current advice.

Vegetarians should be aware that some of the ready-made ingredients used in the recipes in this book might contain animal products. Always check the packaging before use.

Cover images courtesy of iStock and Shutterstock.

CONTENTS

Introduction

It's abundantly clear why slow cooking has been a revered cooking technique since ancient times. It is, quite simply, the best way to produce vegetable dishes with deep flavour and meat so tender it falls from the bone. But with our busy modern lives, who has the time to tend to a pot simmering on the stove all day? Slow cookers are a welcome convenience for anyone who must be out of the house all day, but who wants to return to a delicious, ready-to-eat, home-cooked meal in the evening.

Since its invention in the 1970s, the slow cooker has gained a reputation as a great set-it-and-forget-it gadget for producing finished meals with minimal effort. But the slow cooker isn't just another one-trick appliance providing convenience at the expense of flavour. In fact, it has the ability to produce dishes – from starters to desserts – that taste fantastic. As meat, stock, vegetables and herbs simmer together their flavours emerge, intensify and marry into a whole far more enticing than the individual ingredients might suggest.

The slow cooker is, of course, ideal for making flavour-packed stocks and soups, turning economical cuts of meat into rich stews, and transforming dried beans and hardy vegetables into wholesome meals. But it is also great for cooking more delicate meats, fish and vegetables, because the ingredients are cooked gently, without being broken down. More surprising is that the slow cooker is a great way to cook cakes and other desserts. It comes in handy when you don't want to heat up your kitchen during hot weather or if you are using your oven for something else – a turkey or a roast for a festive dinner.

Moreover, because the slow cooker uses very little electricity (less than a light bulb!), it is both safe and economical to turn it on in the morning and leave it unattended all day. And because the temperature is low and constant, most dishes won't overcook, even after being left for 8 hours or more. What could be better than to arrive home after a long day to be greeted by the enticing aroma of a meal that's ready to eat?

Choosing the right slow cooker for your family

The vast array of slow cookers available is enough to make your head spin. From tiny models to giant pots capable of feeding a small army, each available with or without a myriad options and special features, it can take a bit of research to determine which slow cooker is right for your family.

Quality in any price range

Slow cookers vary widely in price, from the most basic and inexpensive models to high-tech computerized machines that will put a serious dent in your wallet. The good news is that it is possible to find a good-quality slow cooker in any price range. Small models with only the most basic settings are surprisingly affordable. The larger you go and the more bells and whistles you add, the more you can expect to pay.

Size matters

One of the most important considerations in choosing a slow cooker is volume. To determine the size that is right for you, think about how many servings you'll need to make at one time. A 3.8 litre/6½ pint slow cooker is ideal for a family of four or five, while a smaller 1.9 litre/3¼ pint cooker might be perfect for a couple. Larger cookers are great for large families, people who entertain frequently or advance planners who like to cook a big pot of something and freeze leftovers for future meals.

Oval or round?

While for most dishes – soups, stews and the like – the shape of the slow cooker is irrelevant, some dishes are better suited to a particular shape of slow cooker. Oval slow cookers can easily fit big roasts, turkey breasts, leg shanks and other large cuts of meat. On the other hand, if you plan to make a lot of cakes in your slow cooker, a round one is probably a better bet. Give some thought to the types of dish you are most likely to cook in your slow cooker and choose accordingly.

Programmability

The most basic slow cooker models offer only three settings: high, low and off. These models are inexpensive and work just fine. The downside is that they require you to set a separate timer and, more significantly, to be around to turn them off when the cooking time is up.

More expensive models often offer programming features that range from multiple time/temperature settings (such as 'high 4 hours' or 'low 8 hours') to an automatic switch-to-warm feature.

Others allow you to set your own parameters for temperature and timing down to the minute. The more control you have over the settings, the more flexibility you'll get from your cooker – and the more you'll pay for the privilege.

If you plan to use your slow cooker mostly when you will be around the house, a basic model may suit you very well. If, on the other hand, you hope to set your cooker in the morning before heading off to work for the day, consider one that includes a built-in timer and will automatically switch to warm when the time is up.

Versatility

Most slow cookers come with a ceramic cooking vessel that is too porous for use on the hob. There are, however, a few high-end models with cooking inserts that can go from hob to slow cooker and back again. You'll pay a pretty penny for this luxury, but you'll save time and energy by not having to transfer ingredients from one pot to another and, even better, you'll reduce the number of dishes you need to wash.

Portability

Some slow cookers are portable and come fitted with hinged locking lids, carrying handles and specially designed carrying cases and straps to help you transport food safely and easily.

Cleaning, maintenance and safety

Be sure to read the instruction manual that comes with your slow cooker and follow the manufacturer's guidelines for cleaning and maintaining your slow cooker.

While the glass lid of many slow cooker models is dishwasher safe, the ceramic cooking vessel that comes with most models is not. This is because the ceramic material that is used to make the vessel is porous, which is what makes it retain heat. Submerging it in water for long periods will cause it to absorb water, which will have a negative effect on its ability to retain heat. Unless your slow cooker's manual specifically says that it is dishwasher safe, wash it by hand and never leave it submerged in water for any length of time. If you encounter stuck-on food, fill the vessel with warm soapy water and leave it to soak for a few hours, then scrub out the stuck-on food.

Be careful never to plunge the hot ceramic pot into cold water as this sudden temperature change may cause it to crack. Instead, fill it will warm water or, better still, allow the pot to cool before attempting to clean it.

The electric base, of course, should never be submerged in water. To clean it, unplug it and then use a damp sponge or cloth to wipe off any food that may have dripped onto the outside of the cooker.

The outer casing and lid may become very hot during cooking, so do be sure to place the cooker so that it is not too close to or touching any walls, curtains, cords or other potentially flammable items when it is in use. Use oven gloves when touching any part of the slow cooker after it has been on for any period of time.

Always keep refrigerated foods cold until you are ready to add them to the slow cooker. If using frozen meat, poultry, fish or shellfish, it is best to thaw it thoroughly before adding to the slow cooker. If you choose to add it while it is still frozen, you may need to adjust the final cooking time to ensure that the meat is thoroughly cooked.

What to cook in your slow cooker

Slow-cooking certain cuts of meat over a long period of time makes them falling-off-the-bone tender, but you have to be sure to choose the right cuts. Very lean cuts, such as loin or sirloin, will dry out and become stringy in the slow cooker. Fattier cuts, such as chuck, shoulder, shank and rump are better suited to low-and-slow cooking. Likewise, the dark meat portions of poultry (drumsticks, thighs and wings) are better suited to the slow cooker, although breasts can be quite delicious, provided they are browned in a frying pan first, well seasoned and cooked on low.

Of course beans (see Food Safety Note) are also perfect for long, slow cooking. Hearty bean stews and vegetarian chillies, like those made with meat, become thick, rich and deeply flavoured after several hours in the slow cooker.

But it's not just high-protein foods such as meat and beans that are great cooked in the slow cooker. Vegetables, too, turn deeply flavoured and tender after long slow braising. Choose hardy vegetables, such as potatoes, onions, carrots, turnips, winter squashes and fennel. These won't disintegrate with the long slow cooking, but will be fork-tender and rich with the other flavours, herbs and spices included in your recipe.

Food Safety Note

Dried beans cooked in the slow cooker have been linked to food poisoning. To be safe, soak dried beans for at least 5 hours prior to cooking, and then drain and rinse them, place them in a saucepan, cover with cold water, bring to the boil over a medium-high heat and cook at a rapid boil for at least 10 minutes. Remove from the heat, rinse and drain one more time, and then place the beans in the slow cooker, cover with at least 2.5 cm/1 inch of cold water and cook on low, covered, for about 8–10 hours, until tender. To prevent the beans becoming tough, do not add salt until after cooking.

Tips for success with your slow cooker

Don't make the mistake of thinking of your slow cooker as a 'dump-and-go' meal solution. Yes, the slow cooker allows you to 'set-it-and-forget-it', but many foods will benefit greatly from being prepared before going into the slow cooker. For instance, browning meat gives it a caramelized crust that contributes to the overall flavour of the dish and seals in the meat's juices, keeping it from drying out during cooking.

Browning meat before adding it to the slow cooker also renders a good deal of the fat, so it is recommended especially for dishes containing fresh mince, which might otherwise be too greasy.

Likewise, sautéing onions and garlic before adding them to the slow cooker deepens their flavour and, therefore, the taste of the finished dish. Adding spices to the sautéed onions and garlic and allowing them to cook for a moment or two will also help the flavours of the finished dish to marry.

Sometimes you can't wait all day for a dish to cook, and in these instances, cooking on high for a short period of time is appealing. If, however, you've got time to spare and a recipe gives alternative times for cooking on low or high settings, your best bet is usually to choose the longer, slower cooking. The longer and slower your food cooks, the more time it has to develop the depth of flavour that makes it especially delicious.

Bear in mind that, because slow cooker lids are designed to be more or less airtight, sauces and stocks won't reduce the way they do on the hob. For this reason, while it may seem counter-intuitive, adding too much liquid to a dish can render meat dry, vegetables flavourless and sauces bland. Since the slow cooker retains all of the ingredients' natural moisture, a minimal amount of added liquid is sufficient for most dishes.

If, however, you are cooking a dish where you'd like the end result to include a thick sauce, try setting the lid of the slow cooker ajar for the last hour or so of cooking, thus allowing steam to escape and the liquid to reduce. Don't do this too early, however, or you'll lose too much of the heat and your food won't cook through properly.

Cook it slow

All of the recipes in this book are designed to be easy to use – with short ingredient lists and minimal steps – but they never skimp on flavour. Whether your goal is to simplify weekday dinner preparations for your family or to impress guests with a meal that seems to have taken a lot more effort to prepare than it did, you'll find the inspiration and recipes you need right here. Happy slow cooking!

CHAPTER 1
SOUPS & STARTERS

Chicken Noodle Soup 15

Chicken Tortilla Soup 16

New England Clam Chowder 19

Prawn Bisque 20

Salmon Chowder 23

Vietnamese Beef Noodle Soup 24

Tomato & Lentil Soup 27

Italian Bread Soup with Greens 28

Greek Bean & Vegetable Soup 31

Tuscan White Bean Spread with Roasted Garlic 32

Warm Chickpea Salad 35

Pears Stuffed with Blue Cheese 36

Cabbage Roulades 39

Chilli Peppers Stuffed with Turkey 40

Sweet & Sour Chicken Wings 42

Spicy Chicken & Cheese Dip 44

Chicken Quesadillas 47

Mango Beef in Lettuce Cups 48

Beef & Chipotle Burritos 51

Beef Empanadas 52

CHICKEN NOODLE SOUP

serves **4**

1 onion, diced
2 celery sticks, diced
2 carrots, diced
1 kg/2 lb 4 oz oven-ready chicken
700 ml/1½ pints hot chicken stock
115 g/4 oz dried egg tagliatelle
salt and pepper
2 tbsp chopped fresh dill,
   plus extra to garnish

Tales that this soup can cure a cold may be far-fetched but a proper chicken soup is one of the most soul-warming recipes you can make.

1. Place the onion, celery and carrots in the slow cooker. Season the chicken all over with salt and pepper and place on top. Pour the stock over. Cover and cook on low for 5 hours.

2. Leaving the juices in the slow cooker, carefully lift out the chicken and remove the meat from the carcass, discarding the bones and skin. Cut the meat into bite-sized pieces.

3. Skim the excess fat from the juices, then return the chicken to the slow cooker. Turn the setting to high.

4. Bring a large saucepan of lightly salted water to the boil. Add the pasta, bring back to the boil and cook for 8–10 minutes, or until tender but still firm to the bite. Drain, add to the chicken and stir well.

5. Stir the tagliatelle and dill into the slow cooker, cover and cook on high for a further 20 minutes. Garnish with extra dill and serve immediately.

CHICKEN TORTILLA SOUP

serves **4 – 6**

1 tbsp vegetable oil
1 onion, diced
1 tsp chilli powder
1 tsp salt
½ tsp ground cumin
2 tbsp tomato purée
850 ml/1½ pints chicken stock
400 g/14 oz canned chopped tomatoes,
   with juice
1 green chilli, cored, deseeded and
   finely chopped
450 g/1 lb bone-in, skinless
   chicken thighs
40 g/1½ oz tortilla chips, broken into
   small pieces, plus extra to serve

To serve
1 ripe avocado, diced
chopped fresh coriander
1 lime, cut into wedges

*This healthy soup is a hearty first course or
a light meal in a bowl.*

1. Heat the oil in a large frying pan over a medium–high heat.
Add the onion and cook, stirring occasionally, for about
5 minutes, until soft. Add the chilli powder, salt, cumin and
tomato purée and cook, stirring, for a further 1 minute. Add one
third of the stock to the pan and bring to the boil, stirring and
scraping up any brown bits from the base of the pan.

2. Transfer the mixture to the slow cooker. Add the remaining
stock, the tomatoes, chilli, chicken and tortilla chips, then
cover and cook on low for about 4 hours or on high for 8 hours,
until the chicken is cooked through and very tender.

3. Lift out the chicken using a slotted spoon, remove and discard
the bones and shred the meat. Return the chicken to the slow
cooker, cover and heat on high for about 5 minutes, until heated
through. Serve hot, accompanied by diced avocado, chopped
coriander, lime wedges and tortilla chips.

NEW ENGLAND CLAM CHOWDER

serves **4**

25 g/1 oz butter
1 onion, finely chopped
2 potatoes, cut into cubes
1 large carrot, diced
400 ml/14 fl oz fish stock or water
280 g/10 oz canned clams, drained
250 ml/9 fl oz double cream
salt and pepper
chopped fresh parsley, to garnish
fresh crusty bread, to serve

Many recipes for this fish soup exist up and down the east coast of America – some have a creamy consistency while others use tomatoes for colour and flavour.

1. Melt the butter in a frying pan, add the onion and fry over a medium heat for 4–5 minutes, stirring, until golden.

2. Transfer the onion to the slow cooker with the potatoes, carrot, stock and salt and pepper. Cover and cook on high for 3 hours.

3. Add the clams and the cream to the slow cooker and stir to mix evenly. Cover and cook for a further 1 hour.

4. Adjust the seasoning to taste. Transfer to warmed serving bowls, sprinkle with parsley and serve immediately with crusty bread.

PRAWN BISQUE

serves **4 – 6**

1 tbsp butter
1 onion, diced
100 g/3½ oz long-grain rice
2 tbsp tomato purée
1½ tsp salt
½ tsp cayenne pepper
2 litres/3½ pints low-sodium prawn
    stock or fish stock
1 carrot, diced
1 celery stick, diced
225 g/8 oz mushrooms, diced
675 g/1 lb 8 oz raw prawns, shelled,
    deveined and cut into bite-sized
    pieces, if large
150 ml/5 fl oz double cream
2 tbsp lemon juice
snipped chives, to garnish

Thickened with rice, this decadent seafood soup tastes delicious and is also quite healthy.

1. Melt the butter in a large frying pan over a medium–high heat. Add the onion and cook, stirring, for about 5 minutes, until soft. Add the rice, tomato purée, salt and cayenne pepper and cook, stirring, for a further 1 minute. Add a quarter of the stock and cook, stirring, for about 1 minute, scraping up any sediment from the base of the pan.

2. Add the onion mixture to the slow cooker together with the carrot, celery, mushrooms and remaining stock. Cover and cook on high for 3 hours or on low for 6 hours.

3. Using a food processor or blender, purée the soup in batches. Return to the slow cooker, add the prawns, cover and cook on high for 30 minutes, until the prawns are cooked through. Stir in the cream and lemon juice and serve hot, garnished with the chives.

SALMON CHOWDER

serves **4**

15 g/½ oz butter
1 tbsp sunflower oil
1 onion, finely chopped
1 leek, finely chopped
1 fennel bulb, finely chopped,
　feathery tops reserved
280 g/10 oz potatoes, diced
700 ml/1¼ pints fish stock
450 g/1 lb salmon fillet, skinned and
　cut into cubes
300 ml/10 fl oz milk
150 ml/5 fl oz single cream
2 tbsp chopped fresh dill
salt and pepper

Salmon and fennel are the perfect match in this recipe, which would make a great starter for a special dinner. For a family supper the salmon could be replaced by any firm white fish you choose.

1. Melt the butter with the oil in a saucepan. Add the onion, leek and fennel and cook over a low heat, stirring occasionally, for 5 minutes. Add the potatoes and cook, stirring occasionally, for a further 4 minutes, then pour in the stock and season to taste with salt and pepper. Bring to the boil, then transfer to the slow cooker. Cover and cook on low for 3 hours, until the potatoes are tender.

2. Meanwhile, chop the fennel fronds and set aside. Add the salmon to the slow cooker, pour in the milk and stir gently. Re-cover and cook on low for 30 minutes, until the fish flakes easily.

3. Gently stir in the cream, dill and the reserved fennel fronds, re-cover and cook for a further 10–15 minutes, until heated through. Taste and adjust the seasoning, adding salt and pepper if needed. Serve immediately.

VIETNAMESE BEEF
NOODLE SOUP

serves **4**

2 litres/3½ pints beef stock

1 onion, quartered

5-cm/2-inch piece of fresh ginger,
   thickly sliced lengthways

2 cinnamon sticks

3 whole cloves

2 star anise or 1 tsp fennel seeds

2 tbsp Thai fish sauce

1 tsp sugar

450 g/1 lb dried rice noodles

225 g/8 oz top sirloin, very thinly sliced

salt

Accompaniments, to serve

115 g/4 oz beansprouts

lime wedges

chopped fresh herbs, including basil,
   coriander and/or mint

4 spring onions, thinly sliced

2 hot chillies, thinly sliced

You'll find it easier to cut the very thin slices needed for this dish, if you place the meat in the freezer for 15 minutes before slicing.

1. Put the stock, onion, ginger, cinnamon sticks, cloves, star anise, fish sauce and sugar into the slow cooker and stir to combine. Cover and cook on high for 5 hours or on low for 8 hours. Add salt to taste.

2. Pour the liquid through a fine-meshed sieve or a colander lined with muslin and discard the solids. Return the clear stock to the slow cooker and heat on high for about 30 minutes, until very hot, or transfer to a large saucepan and bring to a slow boil over a medium–high heat.

3. Just before serving, cook the noodles according to the packet instructions.

4. Place a few slices of beef in the base of each of four soup bowls and ladle the soup over to lightly cook the beef. Add some noodles to each bowl. Serve immediately with the accompaniments set out in small bowls for diners to help themselves.

TOMATO & LENTIL SOUP

serves **4**

2 tbsp sunflower oil
1 onion, chopped
1 garlic clove, finely chopped
2 celery sticks, chopped
2 carrots, chopped
1 tsp ground cumin
1 tsp ground coriander
175 g/6 oz red or yellow lentils
1 tbsp tomato purée
1.2 litres/2 pints vegetable stock
400 g/14 oz canned chopped tomatoes
1 bay leaf
salt and pepper
crème fraîche and toasted crusty bread,
   to serve

Simple yet satisfying and flavoured with the warm spices of cumin and coriander, basic lentils can be easily transformed into a healthy bowl of soup.

1. Heat the oil in a saucepan. Add the onion and garlic and cook over a low heat, stirring occasionally, for 5 minutes, until softened. Stir in the celery and carrots and cook, stirring occasionally, for a further 4 minutes. Stir in the ground cumin and coriander and cook, stirring, for 1 minute, then add the lentils.

2. Mix the tomato purée with a little of the stock in a small bowl and add to the pan with the remaining stock, the tomatoes and bay leaf. Bring to the boil, then transfer to the slow cooker. Stir well, cover and cook on low for 3½–4 hours.

3. Remove and discard the bay leaf. Transfer the soup to a food processor or blender and process until smooth. Season to taste with salt and pepper. Ladle into warmed soup bowls, top each with a dollop of crème fraîche and serve immediately with toasted crusty bread.

ITALIAN BREAD SOUP WITH GREENS

serves **4**

2 tbsp olive oil

1 onion, diced

1 leek, halved lengthways and
   thinly sliced

2 litres/3½ pints vegetable stock

200 g/7 oz kale, chopped

2 celery sticks, diced

2 carrots, diced

1 tsp crumbled dried oregano

1½ tsp salt

½ tsp pepper

200 g/7 oz day-old cubed
   sourdough bread

30 g/1 oz freshly grated
   Parmesan cheese, to garnish

Turn this healthy, vegetable-packed soup into a one-dish meal by adding a can of cannellini beans along with the vegetables.

1. Heat the oil in a large frying pan over a medium–high heat. Add the onion and leek and sauté for about 5 minutes, until soft.

2. Transfer the mixture to the slow cooker and add the stock, kale, celery, carrots, oregano, salt and pepper. Cover and cook on high for about 4 hours or on low for 8 hours.

3. Add the bread to the soup, cover and cook on high, stirring occasionally, for about 30 minutes, until the bread breaks down and thickens the soup.

4. Serve hot, garnished with the cheese.

GREEK BEAN & VEGETABLE SOUP

serves **4 – 6**

500g/1 lb 2 oz dried haricot beans,
    soaked in cold water overnight
2 onions, finely chopped
2 garlic cloves, finely chopped
2 potatoes, chopped
2 carrots, chopped
2 tomatoes, peeled and chopped
2 celery sticks, chopped
4 tbsp extra virgin olive oil
1 bay leaf
salt and pepper
12 black olives and 2 tbsp snipped chives,
    to garnish

A wonderful recipe when you need something simple and nutritious that requires very little preparation. A great choice for vegetarians too.

1. Drain the beans and rinse well under cold running water. Place the beans in a saucepan, cover with fresh cold water and bring to the boil. Boil rapidly for at least 10 minutes, then remove from the heat, drain and rinse again.

2. Place the beans in the slow cooker and add the onions, garlic, potatoes, carrots, tomatoes, celery, olive oil and bay leaf.

3. Pour in 2 litres/3½ pints boiling water, making sure that all the ingredients are fully submerged. Cover and cook on low for 12 hours until the beans are tender.

4. Remove and discard the bay leaf. Season the soup to taste with salt and pepper and garnish with the olives and chives. Transfer into warm soup bowls and serve.

TUSCAN WHITE BEAN SPREAD WITH ROASTED GARLIC

serves **6 – 8**

1 garlic bulb
3 tbsp olive oil
400 g/14 oz canned cannellini beans,
    rinsed and drained
2 tbsp lemon juice
2 tsp finely chopped fresh rosemary
1/8–1/4 tsp cayenne pepper,
    plus extra to taste
85 g/3 oz freshly grated
    Parmesan cheese
salt
baguette slices, to serve

Slow cooking is an easy way to roast garlic, giving it an enticing mellow and savoury caramelized flavor, without having to tend it while it cooks.

1. Keeping the garlic bulb intact, slice about 1 cm/1/2 inch off the top, exposing the cloves. Fill the slow cooker with water to a depth of about 5 mm/1/4 inch. Stand the garlic bulb cut side up in the slow cooker and drizzle 1 tablespoon of the oil over the top. Cover and cook on low for about 6 hours, until the garlic is soft and golden brown. Remove the garlic, leave to cool, then squeeze the cloves into a small bowl.

2. Put the beans, half of the roasted garlic (reserve the remaining garlic for another recipe), lemon juice, rosemary, cayenne pepper and 1/4 teaspoon of salt into a food processor and process until smooth.

3. Add the cheese and pulse until well combined. If the mixture is too thick, add 1–2 tablespoons of water and pulse to incorporate. Taste and add more salt and cayenne pepper if necessary. Serve with baguette slices.

WARM CHICKPEA SALAD

serves **6**

225 g/8 oz dried chickpeas,
    soaked overnight in cold
    water and drained
115 g/4 oz stoned black olives
4 spring onions, finely chopped
fresh parsley sprigs, to garnish
crusty bread, to serve

Dressing
2 tbsp red wine vinegar
2 tbsp mixed chopped fresh herbs,
    such as parsley, rosemary and thyme
3 garlic cloves, very finely chopped
125 ml/4 fl oz extra virgin olive oil
salt and pepper

A great starter served warm, but equally tasty if you chill and serve cold. As a variation, you could add flaked, canned tuna and serve piled in jacket potatoes.

1. Place the chickpeas in the slow cooker and add sufficient boiling water to cover. Cover and cook on low for 12 hours.

2. Drain well and transfer to a bowl. Stir in the olives and spring onions.

3. To make the dressing, whisk together the vinegar, herbs and garlic in a jug and season with salt and pepper to taste. Gradually whisk in the olive oil. Pour the dressing over the still-warm chickpeas and toss lightly to coat. Garnish with the parsley sprigs and serve warm with crusty bread.

PEARS STUFFED WITH BLUE CHEESE

serves **4**

2 just-ripe pears
115 g/4 oz Gorgonzola cheese
or other blue cheese
1 tbsp honey
30 g/1 oz pecan nuts or walnuts,
chopped

Use spiced, candied nuts instead of plain chopped nuts for a sophisticated touch.

1. Fill the slow cooker with water to a depth of about 2.5 cm/1 inch.

2. Halve the pears lengthways and scoop out the core. Slice off a bit from the outside of each pear half to make a flat surface so that the pears will sit level when placed in the slow cooker.

3. Divide the cheese equally between the pears, pressing it into the hollows. Place the pears cheese side up in the slow cooker in a single layer and drizzle the honey evenly over the pears. Cover and cook on high for about 2 hours, until the pears are soft.

4. Remove the pears from the slow cooker with a slotted spoon and arrange on a serving plate. Sprinkle the nuts evenly over the pears. If liked, brown the pears under the grill for 1–2 minutes. Serve hot.

CABBAGE ROULADES

serves **6**

225 g/8 oz mixed nuts, finely ground
2 onions, finely chopped
1 garlic clove, finely chopped
2 celery sticks, finely chopped
115 g/4 oz Cheddar cheese, grated
1 tsp finely chopped fresh thyme
2 eggs
1 tsp yeast extract
12 large green cabbage leaves

Tomato sauce
2 tbsp sunflower oil
2 onions, chopped
2 garlic cloves, finely chopped
600 g/1 lb 5 oz canned chopped
　　tomatoes
2 tbsp tomato purée
1½ tsp sugar
1 bay leaf
salt and pepper

1. To make the tomato sauce, heat the oil in a heavy-based saucepan. Add the onions and cook over a medium heat, stirring occasionally, for 5 minutes, until softened. Stir in the garlic and cook for 1 minute, then add the tomatoes, tomato purée, sugar and bay leaf. Season to taste with salt and pepper and bring to the boil. Reduce the heat and simmer gently for 20 minutes, until thickened.

2. Meanwhile, mix together the nuts, onions, garlic, celery, cheese and thyme in a bowl. Lightly beat the eggs with the yeast extract in a jug, then stir into the nut mixture. Set aside.

3. Cut out the thick stalk from the cabbage leaves. Blanch the leaves in a large saucepan of boiling water for 5 minutes, then drain and refresh under cold water. Pat dry with kitchen paper.

4. Place a little of the nut mixture on the stalk end of each cabbage leaf. Fold the sides over, then roll up to make a neat parcel.

5. Arrange the parcels in the slow cooker, seam-side down. Remove and discard the bay leaf from the tomato sauce and pour the sauce over the cabbage rolls. Cover and cook on low for 3–4 hours. Serve the cabbage roulades hot or cold.

CHILLI PEPPERS STUFFED WITH TURKEY

4 large poblano or pasilla chillies
1 tbsp vegetable oil
1 onion, diced
450 g/1 lb fresh turkey mince
1 tsp ground cumin
1 tsp mild chilli powder
1 tsp crumbled dried oregano
1 tsp salt
225 ml/8 fl oz salsa, hot or mild to taste
115 g/4 oz mature Cheddar cheese,
    grated
4 large eggs, lightly beaten
2 tbsp plain flour
175 ml/6 fl oz canned evaporated milk

This flavoursome dish is an easy and healthy version of the traditional Mexican speciality, chilli rellenos.

1. Preheat the grill to high. Put the chillies on a baking sheet, place under the preheated grill and cook for 3–5 minutes on each side, until the skin begins to blister and blacken. Remove from the grill, place in a bowl, and cover with clingfilm. Leave to steam for about 10 minutes, until cool enough to handle, then peel off the skins. Make a slit down one side of each chilli to open it up and remove the stem and seeds.

2. Heat the oil in a large frying pan over a medium–high heat. Add the onion and cook, stirring, for about 5 minutes, until soft. Add the turkey and cook, breaking up the meat with a wooden spoon, for about 4 minutes, or until brown. Stir in the cumin, chilli powder, oregano and salt and cook for a further 1 minute. Stir in the salsa and three quarters of the cheese.

3. Lay the chillies cut side up on a work surface. Stuff them with the turkey mixture, dividing the mixture equally between them. Place the stuffed chillies in the slow cooker in a single layer.

4. Put the eggs, flour and evaporated milk into a mixing bowl and whisk together. Pour the egg mixture over the chillies and top with the remaining cheese. Cover and cook on low for 2 hours, until puffed and golden brown. Serve hot.

SWEET & SOUR CHICKEN WINGS

serves **4 – 6**

1 kg/2 lb 4 oz chicken wings,
   tips removed

2 celery sticks, chopped

700 ml/1¼ pints hot chicken stock

2 tbsp cornflour

3 tbsp white wine vinegar or rice vinegar

3 tbsp dark soy sauce

5 tbsp sweet chilli sauce

55 g/2 oz soft light brown sugar

400 g/14 oz canned pineapple
   chunks in juice, drained

200 g/7 oz canned sliced bamboo shoots,
   drained and rinsed

½ green pepper, deseeded and
   thinly sliced

½ red pepper, deseeded and thinly sliced

salt

steamed pak choi, to serve

1. Put the chicken wings and celery in the slow cooker and season well with salt. Pour in the stock, cover and cook on low for 5 hours.

2. Drain the chicken wings, reserving 350 ml/12 fl oz of the stock, and keep warm. Pour the reserved stock into a saucepan and stir in the cornflour. Add the vinegar, soy sauce and chilli sauce. Place over a medium heat and stir in the sugar. Cook, stirring constantly, for 5 minutes, or until the sugar has dissolved completely and the sauce is thickened, smooth and clear.

3. Reduce the heat, stir in the pineapple, bamboo shoots and peppers and simmer gently for 2–3 minutes. Stir in the chicken wings until they are thoroughly coated, then transfer to warmed serving bowls. Serve immediately with pak choi.

SPICY CHICKEN & CHEESE DIP

serves **6 – 8**

450 g/1 lb Gouda cheese, coarsely grated
225 g/8 oz cooked chicken breast, diced
225 ml/8 fl oz chunky salsa,
 hot or mild to taste
225 ml/8 fl oz soured cream
3 spring onions, thinly sliced, to garnish
chopped fresh coriander, to garnish
tortilla chips, to serve

This spicy dip will get any fiesta off to the right start. Use spicy salsa if you like a kick, or keep it tame with a milder version.

1. Put the cheese, chicken and salsa into the slow cooker, stir to mix well, cover and cook on low for 2 hours.

2. Stir in the soured cream, re-cover and cook on high for a further 20 minutes, until heated through.

3. Serve hot, garnished with the spring onions and coriander, with tortilla chips for dipping.

CHICKEN QUESADILLAS

serves **4**

4 skinless, boneless chicken breasts
$\frac{1}{2}$ tsp crushed dried chillies
2 garlic cloves, crushed
2 tbsp finely chopped parsley
2 tbsp olive oil
350 g/12 oz cherry tomatoes
4 large wheat tortillas
250 g/9 oz mozzarella cheese
salt and pepper

Quesadillas are toasted tortilla wraps with cheese inside. You can create many delicious fillings including this spicy marinated chicken mix.

1. Place the chicken in a bowl with the chillies, garlic, parsley and 1 tbsp olive oil, and turn to coat evenly. Cover and leave in the refrigerator to marinate for at least 1 hour, or overnight.

2. Tip the tomatoes into the slow cooker and arrange the chicken breasts on top. Season with salt and pepper. Cover and cook on high for 2 hours, until tender.

3. Remove the chicken and shred the meat using two forks. Place on one side of each tortilla and top with the tomatoes. Chop or tear the mozzarella and arrange on top. Moisten the edges of the tortillas and fold over to enclose the filling.

4. Brush a griddle or large frying pan with the remaining oil and place over a medium heat. Add the quesadillas to the pan and cook until golden, turning once. Cut into wedges and serve. Any spare juices can be spooned over.

MANGO BEEF IN LETTUCE CUPS

serves **6 – 8**

675 g/1 lb 8 oz chuck steak,
   cut into 1-cm/¹/₂-inch dice
1 tbsp cornflour
1 fresh mango, peeled, stoned and diced
2 hot red chillies, cored and diced
2 tbsp soy sauce
2 tbsp mirin or other sweet white wine
2 tbsp moist brown sugar
1 tsp sesame oil
cup-shaped lettuce leaves, to serve

*This unusual starter offers a tantalizing
combination of sweet and spicy flavours.*

1. Put the beef and the cornflour into the slow cooker and toss to
coat the beef evenly. Add the mango and chillies and stir to mix.
Add the soy sauce, mirin, sugar and oil and stir to mix well.

2. Cover and cook on high for about 1 hour, then set the lid slightly
ajar and continue to cook on high for a further 1 hour, until the
meat is tender and the sauce has thickened.

3. Transfer the meat to a serving bowl and serve with the lettuce
leaves, so that diners can scoop some of the meat into a lettuce
cup and wrap it up like a taco.

BEEF & CHIPOTLE BURRITOS

serves **4**

1 tbsp olive oil
1 onion, sliced
600 g/1 lb 5 oz chuck steak
1 dried chipotle pepper, soaked in
   boiling water for 20 minutes
1 garlic clove, crushed
1 tsp ground cumin
400 g/14 oz canned chopped tomatoes
8 large tortillas
salt and pepper
soured cream and green salad, to serve

Chipotle peppers are smoked, dried, jalapeño chillies, which have been used in Mexican cooking for centuries. In this recipe they add the heat to a spicy beef filling for tortillas.

1. Heat the oil in a pan and fry the onion for 3–4 minutes until golden. Tip into the slow cooker and arrange the beef on top. Drain and chop the chipotle. Sprinkle the garlic, cumin, tomatoes, salt and pepper over the meat.

2. Cover and cook on low for 4 hours, until the meat is tender.

3. Warm the tortillas. Remove the beef and shred with a fork. Divide between the tortillas and spoon over the sauce. Wrap, and serve with soured cream and green salad.

BEEF EMPANADAS

makes about **30**

1 tbsp vegetable oil
1 onion, finely chopped
1 garlic clove, finely chopped
450 g/1lb extra lean fresh beef mince
1 tsp salt
1 tsp ground cumin
1 tsp chilli powder
1 tsp dried oregano or 1 tbsp finely
    chopped fresh oregano
1 red pepper, cored, deseeded and diced
70 g/2½ oz pimiento-stuffed
    green olives, chopped
40 g/1½ oz sultanas
2 tbsp tomato purée
450 g/1 lb ready-made shortcrust pastry
flour for dusting

These savoury bites are always a hit at parties. Freeze a batch before baking, and be ready for a fiesta at a moment's notice.

1. Heat the oil in a large frying pan over a medium–high heat. Add the onion and garlic and cook, stirring, for about 5 minutes, until soft. Add the beef and cook, stirring, until brown. Drain off the excess fat and discard. Add the salt, cumin, chilli powder and oregano and continue to cook, stirring, for a further minute, then transfer to the slow cooker.

2. Add the red pepper, olives, sultanas and tomato purée and stir to combine. Cover and cook on low for 4 hours.

3. Preheat the oven to 200°C/400°F/Gas Mark 6 and line a baking tray with baking paper. Roll out the pastry on a lightly floured surface and cut it into 6-cm/2½ -inch rounds with a pastry cutter. Place about 1 tablespoon of the filling on each round, fold over the pastry and crimp the edges together to seal each pie.

4. Place the finished empanadas on the prepared baking tray and bake in the preheated oven for 20–25 minutes, until golden brown. Remove from the oven and transfer to a wire rack to cool slightly. Serve warm.

CHAPTER 2

EVERYDAY EATING

Chicken & Apple Pot 57

Chicken with Olives & Sun-dried Tomatoes 58

Chicken & Mushroom Stew 60

Chicken Paprika 62

Easy Chinese Chicken 65

Turkey Chilli with Sweet Potatoes 66

Turkey Hash 69

Chinese-style Barbecue Pork 70

Spicy Pulled Pork 73

Korean Braised Beef Ribs 74

Chunky Beef Chilli 77

Shredded Beef with Tzatziki Sauce 78

Beef Ragù with Tagliatelle 81

Moroccan Spiced Beef Stew 82

Traditional Pot Roast 85

Thai Beef Curry 86

Ginger-steamed Halibut with Tomatoes & Beans 88

Jambalaya 91

Salmon with Leeks & Cream 92

Tagliatelle with Tuna 95

CHICKEN & APPLE POT

serves **4**

1 tbsp olive oil

4 chicken portions,
   about 175 g/6 oz each

1 onion, chopped

2 celery sticks, roughly chopped

1½ tbsp plain flour

300 ml/10 fl oz clear apple juice

150 ml/5 fl oz chicken stock

1 cooking apple, cored and
   cut into quarters

2 bay leaves

1–2 tsp clear honey

1 yellow pepper, deseeded and
   cut into chunks

salt and pepper

To garnish

1 large or 2 medium eating apples,
   cored and sliced

1 tbsp melted butter

2 tbsp demerara sugar

1 tbsp chopped fresh mint

Chicken and apples go together so well. In this recipe the soft, melting cooking apple adds sharpness while the garnish of caramelized eating apples gives sweetness and crunch.

1. Heat the oil in a heavy-based frying pan. Add the chicken and cook over a medium–high heat, turning frequently, for 10 minutes, until golden brown. Transfer to the slow cooker. Add the onion and celery to the pan and cook over a low heat for 5 minutes, until softened. Sprinkle in the flour and cook for 2 minutes, then remove the pan from the heat.

2. Gradually stir in the apple juice and stock, then return the pan to the heat and bring to the boil. Stir in the cooking apple, bay leaves and honey and season to taste. Pour the mixture over the chicken in the slow cooker, cover and cook on low for 6½ hours, until the chicken is tender and cooked through. Stir in the pepper, re-cover and cook on high for 45 minutes.

3. Shortly before serving, preheat the grill. Brush one side of the eating apple slices with half the melted butter and sprinkle with half the sugar. Cook under the preheated grill for 2–3 minutes, until the sugar has caramelized. Turn the slices over with tongs, brush with the remaining butter and sprinkle with the remaining sugar. Grill for a further 2 minutes. Transfer the stew to warmed plates and garnish with the caramelized apple slices and the mint. Serve immediately.

CHICKEN WITH OLIVES & SUN-DRIED TOMATOES

serves **4**

900 g/2 lb skinless, bone-in chicken
  thighs, drumsticks, or a combination
1 tsp salt
½ tsp pepper
30 g/1 oz plain flour
2 tbsp olive oil, plus extra if needed
1 onion, diced
3 garlic cloves, finely chopped
125 ml/4 fl oz dry white wine
800 g/1 lb 12 oz canned chopped
  tomatoes
115 g/4 oz stoned Kalamata olives,
  quartered
75 g/2¾ oz sun-dried tomatoes, chopped
fresh basil leaves, to garnish
cooked pasta, to serve

With easy preparation and a long cooking time, this chicken stew offers a taste of Provence with minimal effort.

1. Season the chicken with half the salt and the pepper. Place the flour in a polythene bag, add the chicken pieces, in batches, if necessary, then hold the top securely closed and shake well to coat.

2. Heat the oil in a large frying pan over a medium–high heat. Add the chicken pieces and cook on one side for about 4 minutes, until brown. Turn and cook on the other side for about 4 minutes, until brown. Place the chicken in the slow cooker.

3. Add some more oil to the pan if needed, then add the onion and garlic and sauté over a medium heat for 15 minutes, until soft. Add the wine and bring to the boil. Cook, stirring and scraping up any sediment from the base of the pan, for about 2 minutes. Add the canned tomatoes, olives, sun-dried tomatoes and the remaining salt and cook, stirring, for about 1 minute.

4. Add the mixture to the slow cooker on top of the chicken. Cover and cook on high for 4 hours or on low for 8 hours. Serve hot with pasta, garnished with basil.

CHICKEN & MUSHROOM STEW

serves **4**

15 g/½ oz unsalted butter

2 tbsp olive oil

1.8 kg/4 lb skinless chicken portions

2 red onions, sliced

2 garlic cloves, finely chopped

400 g/14 oz canned chopped tomatoes

2 tbsp chopped fresh flat-leaf parsley

6 fresh basil leaves, torn

1 tbsp sun-dried tomato purée

150 ml/5 fl oz red wine

225 g/8 oz mushrooms, sliced

salt and pepper

An ideal recipe for a family supper but also a great choice for a dinner with friends. Experiment with the wide variety of mushrooms available in your supermarket.

1. Heat the butter and oil in a heavy-based frying pan. Add the chicken, in batches if necessary, and cook over a medium–high heat, turning frequently, for 10 minutes, until golden brown all over. Using a slotted spoon, transfer the chicken to the slow cooker.

2. Add the onions and garlic to the frying pan and cook over a low heat, stirring occasionally, for 10 minutes, until golden. Add the tomatoes with their can juices, stir in the parsley, basil, tomato purée and wine and season with salt and pepper. Bring to the boil, then pour the mixture over the chicken.

3. Cover the slow cooker and cook on low for 6½ hours. Stir in the mushrooms, re-cover and cook on high for 30 minutes, until the chicken is tender and the vegetables are cooked through. Taste and adjust the seasoning if necessary and serve immediately.

CHICKEN PAPRIKA

serves **4**

900 g/2 lb skinless, bone-in chicken
    thighs or drumsticks, or a combination
1 teaspoon salt
$\frac{1}{2}$ teaspoon pepper
70 g/2$\frac{1}{2}$ oz plain flour
2 tbsp vegetable oil
1 tbsp butter
1 large onion, diced
3 tbsp paprika
2 tbsp tomato purée
225 ml/8 fl oz chicken stock
125 ml/4 fl oz soured cream
finely chopped fresh dill, to garnish
cooked egg noodles or dumplings,
    to serve

This hearty chicken stew, brightened with paprika and enriched with soured cream, will warm you right through on a cold night.

1. Season the chicken with $\frac{1}{2}$ teaspoon of salt and $\frac{1}{2}$ teaspoon of pepper. Place the flour in a polythene bag, add the chicken pieces, in batches, if necessary, then hold the top securely closed and shake well to coat.

2. Heat the oil in a large frying pan over a medium–high heat. Add the chicken pieces and cook on one side for about 4 minutes, until brown. Turn and cook on the other side for about 4 minutes, until brown. Place the chicken in the slow cooker.

3. Add the butter to the pan and heat over a medium–high heat, until melted. Add the onion and cook, stirring occasionally, for about 5 minutes, until soft. Add the paprika, tomato purée and the remaining salt, and cook, stirring, for about 1 minute.

4. Add the stock and bring to the boil, stirring and scraping up the sediment from the base of the pan. Cook for about 1 minute, then pour the onion mixture into the slow cooker over the chicken pieces. Cover and cook on high for 6 hours or on low for 9 hours.

5. Just before serving, stir in the soured cream. Garnish with dill and serve with noodles.

EASY CHINESE CHICKEN

serves **4**

2 tsp grated fresh ginger

4 garlic cloves, finely chopped

2 star anise

150 ml / 5 fl oz Chinese rice
   wine or medium dry sherry

2 tbsp dark soy sauce

1 tsp sesame oil

5 tbsp water

4 skinless chicken thighs or drumsticks

shredded spring onions, to garnish

cooked rice, to serve

This great-tasting Chinese recipe can be served simply with steamed rice or as part of a more elaborate meal with the addition of a quickly cooked stir-fried vegetable selection.

1. Mix together the ginger, garlic, star anise, rice wine, soy sauce, sesame oil and water in a bowl. Place the chicken in a saucepan, add the spice mixture and bring to the boil.

2. Transfer to the slow cooker, cover and cook on low for 4 hours, or until the chicken is tender and cooked through.

3. Remove and discard the star anise. Transfer the chicken to warmed serving plates, garnish with shredded spring onions and serve immediately with rice.

TURKEY CHILLI WITH SWEET POTATOES

serves **4 – 6**

1 tbsp vegetable oil
1 onion, diced
675 g/1 lb 8 oz fresh turkey mince
70 g/2½ oz tomato purée
1 tbsp mild chilli powder
1 tsp ground cumin
2 canned chipotle chillies in adobo sauce,
    deseeded and diced, plus 2 teaspoons
    of the adobo sauce (or substitute
    1 tsp ground chipotles)
1 tsp salt
400 g/14 oz canned chopped tomatoes
450 ml/16 fl oz chicken stock
1 large sweet potato (about 225 g/8 oz),
    diced

To serve
fresh coriander
soured cream
grated Cheddar cheese
diced avocado
finely chopped red onion

Add a can of black beans along with the sweet potatoes to feed a crowd and make this healthy chilli even better for you.

1. Heat the oil in a large frying pan. Add the onion and cook, stirring, for about 5 minutes, until soft. Add the turkey and cook, breaking up the meat with a wooden spoon, for about 4 minutes, until brown. Stir in the tomato purée, chilli powder, cumin, chillies and adobo sauce, and salt and cook for a further 1 minute.

2. Transfer the mixture to the slow cooker. Stir in the tomatoes, stock and sweet potato. Cover and cook on high for 4 hours or on low for 8 hours. Serve hot, accompanied by the coriander, soured cream, cheese, avocado and red onion.

TURKEY HASH

serves **4**

1 tbsp olive oil
500 g/1 lb 2 oz turkey mince
1 large red onion, diced
550 g/1 lb 4 oz butternut squash, diced
2 celery sticks, sliced
500 g/1 lb 2 oz potatoes, diced
3 tbsp Worcestershire sauce
2 bay leaves
salt and pepper

This is a great-tasting combination as the slightly sweet, nutty flavour of the squash complements the rich turkey. Squash also keeps its shape well in the slow cooker.

1. Heat the oil in a frying pan, add the turkey and fry over a high heat, stirring, until broken up and lightly browned.

2. Place all the vegetables in the slow cooker then add the turkey and pan juices. Add the Worcestershire sauce and bay leaves and season with salt and pepper. Cover and cook on low for 7 hours. Transfer to warmed serving bowls and serve immediately.

CHINESE-STYLE BARBECUE PORK

serves **4 – 6**

2 garlic cloves, finely chopped
1 tbsp finely chopped fresh ginger
2 tbsp honey
2 tbsp soy sauce
2 tbsp mirin or other sweet white wine
1 tsp sesame oil
1 tsp Chinese five-spice powder
900 g/2 lb pork shoulder,
    boned and rolled
3 spring onions, thinly sliced, to garnish
steamed rice, to serve

This easy, set-it-and-forget-it pork dish has all the sweet and savoury flavour of slow-cooked Chinese pork.

1. Put the garlic, ginger, honey, soy sauce, mirin, oil and five-spice powder into a large bowl and stir to mix. Add the pork and stir to coat. Cover and refrigerate for at least 2 hours or overnight.

2. Place the pork and the marinade in the slow cooker. Cover and cook on high for 6 hours or on low for 10 hours, until the meat is very tender.

3. Slice the meat and then pull into shreds using two forks. Garnish with spring onions and serve hot with rice.

SPICY PULLED PORK

serves **4**

2 onions, sliced
1.5 kg/3 lb 5 oz boned and rolled
   pork shoulder
2 tbsp demerara sugar
2 tbsp Worcestershire sauce
1 tbsp American mustard
2 tbsp tomato ketchup
1 tbsp cider vinegar
salt and pepper
hamburger buns or ciabatta rolls,
   to serve

Have your own hog roast at home! Slow cooking creates pork that's deliciously moist, tender and full of flavour for the ultimate sandwich everyone will love.

1. Put the onions in the slow cooker and place the pork on top. Mix the sugar, Worcestershire sauce, mustard, ketchup and vinegar together and spread all over the surface of the pork. Season to taste with salt and pepper. Cover and cook on low for 8 hours.

2. Remove the pork from the slow cooker and use two forks to pull it apart into shreds.

3. Skim any excess fat from the juices and stir a little juice into the pork. Serve in hamburger buns, with the remaining juices for spooning over.

KOREAN BRAISED BEEF RIBS

serves **4 – 6**

1 onion, diced
3 garlic cloves, finely chopped
1 tbsp finely chopped fresh ginger
2 tbsp soy sauce
2 tbsp soft dark brown sugar
2 tbsp mirin or other sweet white wine
1 tbsp sesame oil
1 tsp chilli paste
1.25 kg/2 lb 12 oz bone-in beef short ribs
2 small potatoes, cubed
2 carrots, cubed
3 spring onions, thinly sliced, to garnish
1 tbsp toasted sesame seeds, to garnish
steamed rice, to serve

If possible, ask your butcher to cut the ribs into 7.5-cm/3-inch lengths to make serving easier.

1. Put the onion, garlic, ginger, soy sauce, sugar, mirin, oil and chilli paste into a bowl large enough to hold the meat and stir to combine. Add the ribs and turn to coat in the mixture. Cover and place in the refrigerator to marinate for at least 2 hours or overnight.

2. Place the beef, together with the marinade, in the slow cooker. Add the potatoes and carrots and stir to mix. Cover and cook on high for about 6 hours or on low for about 9 hours, until the meat is tender and falling off the bone.

3. Serve hot, garnished with the spring onions and sesame seeds, with steamed rice.

CHUNKY BEEF CHILLI

serves **4**

250 g/9 oz dried red kidney beans,
   soaked overnight
600 ml/1 pint water
2 garlic cloves, chopped
5 tbsp tomato purée
1 small green chilli, chopped
2 tsp ground cumin
2 tsp ground coriander
600 g/1 lb 5 oz chuck steak, diced
1 large onion, chopped
1 large green pepper, deseeded
   and sliced
salt and pepper
soured cream, to serve

Chunks of beef, onions, garlic and green pepper are cooked with chilli to give just the right amount of kick. Serve with rice, tortilla chips and guacamole for a satisfying meal.

1. Drain and rinse the beans, place in a saucepan, add enough water to cover and bring to a boil. Boil rapidly for 10 minutes, then remove from the heat and drain and rinse again. Place the beans in the slow cooker and add 600 ml/1 pint cold water.

2. Mix the garlic, tomato purée, chilli, cumin and coriander together in a large bowl. Add the steak, onion and green pepper and mix to coat evenly.

3. Place the meat and vegetables on top of the beans, cover and cook on low for 9 hours, until the beans and meat are tender. Stir and season to taste with salt and pepper.

4. Transfer to warmed serving bowls and top with a swirl of soured cream. Serve immediately.

SHREDDED BEEF WITH TZATZIKI SAUCE

serves **4**

3 tbsp natural yogurt

1 tbsp lemon juice

2 garlic cloves, finely chopped

1 tsp crumbled dried oregano or
   1 tbsp chopped fresh oregano

¾ tsp salt

½ tsp pepper

675 g/1 lb 8 oz chuck steak, diced

Sauce

1 cucumber, peeled, deseeded and
   coarsely grated

1 tsp salt

225 ml/8 fl oz natural yogurt

3 tbsp lemon juice

50 g/1¾ oz chopped fresh mint leaves

To serve

4 rounds warmed flatbread or pitta

1 large tomato, cut into wedges

115 g/4 oz shredded lettuce

Make this into a more traditionally Greek filling by using lamb instead of beef.

1. Put the yogurt, lemon juice, garlic, oregano, salt and pepper into the slow cooker and stir to mix well. Add the beef and turn to coat. Cover and cook on high for about 5 hours or on low for about 9 hours, until the beef is tender. Shred the beef and mix it with the cooking juices.

2. To make the sauce, place the cucumber on a double layer of kitchen paper and sprinkle with ½ teaspoon of the salt. Set aside. Put the yogurt, the remaining salt, lemon juice and mint into a medium-sized bowl and stir to combine. Wrap the cucumber in the kitchen paper and squeeze out the excess juice over the sink. Mix the cucumber into the yogurt mixture.

3. Serve the shredded beef on flatbread, drizzled with the sauce and topped with tomato wedges and shredded lettuce.

BEEF RAGÙ WITH TAGLIATELLE

serves **6**

3 tbsp olive oil

85 g/3 oz pancetta or bacon, diced

1 onion, chopped

1 garlic clove, finely chopped

1 carrot, chopped

1 celery stick, chopped

450 g/1 lb minced steak

125 ml/4 fl oz red wine

2 tbsp tomato purée

400 g/14 oz canned chopped tomatoes

300 ml/10 fl oz beef stock

½ tsp dried oregano

1 bay leaf

450 g/1 lb dried tagliatelle

salt and pepper

grated Parmesan cheese, to serve

Probably the most popular accompaniment to simply cooked pasta. Long, slow cooking creates a rich-tasting sauce that coats and clings to the tagliatelle.

1. Heat the oil in a saucepan. Add the pancetta and cook over a medium heat, stirring frequently, for 3 minutes. Reduce the heat, add the onion, garlic, carrot and celery and cook, stirring occasionally, for 5 minutes, until the vegetables have softened.

2. Increase the heat to medium and add the minced steak. Cook, stirring frequently and breaking it up with a wooden spoon, for 8–10 minutes, until evenly browned. Pour in the wine and cook for a few minutes, until the alcohol has evaporated, then stir in the tomato purée, tomatoes, stock, oregano and bay leaf and season to taste with salt and pepper.

3. Bring to the boil, then transfer the ragù to the slow cooker. Cover and cook on low for 8–8½ hours.

4. Shortly before serving, bring a large saucepan of lightly salted water to the boil. Add the pasta, bring back to the boil and cook for 8–10 minutes, until tender but still firm to the bite. Drain and tip into a warmed serving bowl. Remove and discard the bay leaf, then add the ragù to the pasta. Toss with two forks, sprinkle with the Parmesan and serve immediately.

MOROCCAN SPICED BEEF STEW

serves **4 – 6**

2 tbsp vegetable oil
1 onion, diced
1½ tsp salt
½ tsp pepper
2 tsp ground cumin
½ tsp ground cinnamon
½ tsp ground ginger
225 ml/8 fl oz red wine
675 g/1 lb 8 oz chuck steak,
   cut into 5-cm/2-inch pieces
130 g/4¾ oz dried apricots, diced
2 tbsp honey
125 ml/4 fl oz water
chopped fresh coriander, to garnish
cooked couscous, to serve

Heady spices and sweet dried apricots come together for an exotic twist on beef stew.

1. Heat the oil in a large frying pan. Add the onion and cook, stirring, for about 5 minutes, until soft. Add the salt, pepper, cumin, cinnamon and ginger and cook, stirring, for a further 1 minute.

2. Add the wine, bring to the boil and cook for 1 minute, scraping up any sediment from the base of the pan. Transfer the mixture to the slow cooker.

3. Add the beef, apricots, honey and water and stir to mix. Cover and cook on high for 6 hours or on low for 9 hours, until the meat is very tender.

4. Serve hot with couscous, garnished with coriander.

TRADITIONAL POT ROAST

serves **6**

1 onion, finely chopped

4 carrots, sliced

4 baby turnips, sliced

4 celery sticks, sliced

2 potatoes, sliced

1 sweet potato, sliced

1.3–1.8 kg/3–4 lb topside of beef,
   in one piece

1 bouquet garni

300 ml/10 fl oz hot beef stock

salt and pepper

The ultimate one-pot roast that produces tender meat and perfectly cooked vegetables. The cooking juices can be thickened with cornflour if you prefer.

1. Place the onion, carrots, turnips, celery, potatoes and sweet potato in the slow cooker and stir to mix well.

2. Rub the beef all over with salt and pepper, then place on top of the bed of vegetables. Add the bouquet garni and pour in the stock. Cover and cook on low for 9–10 hours, until the beef is cooked to your liking. Serve immediately.

THAI BEEF CURRY

serves **4**

75 g/2¾ oz Thai red curry paste
175 ml/6 fl oz unsweetened coconut milk
50 g/1¾ oz soft dark brown sugar
1 tbsp Thai fish sauce
75 g/2¾ oz smooth peanut butter
900 g/2 lb chuck steak,
   cut into 2.5-cm/1-inch dice
2 potatoes, diced
125 ml/4 fl oz beef stock or water
fresh basil leaves, cut into ribbons,
   to garnish
steamed rice, to serve

Enriched with coconut milk and peanut butter, this simple curry will transport you to Southeast Asia.

1. Put the curry paste, coconut milk, sugar, fish sauce and peanut butter into the slow cooker and stir to combine. Add the beef, potatoes and stock and stir to coat in the mixture.

2. Cover and cook on high for about 4 hours or on low for 8 hours, then set the lid slightly ajar and cook for a further 1 hour, or until the beef is very tender and the sauce has thickened slightly. Serve hot, garnished with basil, with the steamed rice.

GINGER-STEAMED HALIBUT WITH TOMATOES & BEANS

serves **4**

1 tbsp finely chopped fresh ginger

2 garlic cloves, finely chopped

1–2 hot red chillies, cored,
    deseeded and diced

2 tbsp Thai fish sauce

2 tbsp mirin or other sweet white wine

1 tsp sugar

4 halibut fillets (about 675 g/
    1 lb 8 oz in total)

vegetable oil, for oiling

350 g/12 oz French beans,
    topped and tailed

450 g/1 lb cherry tomatoes, halved,
    or quartered if large

To garnish

4 spring onions, thinly sliced

finely chopped fresh coriander

fresh basil leaves, shredded

This light and healthy main dish takes only minutes to prepare but is full of flavour.

1. Put the ginger, garlic, chillies, fish sauce, mirin and sugar into a baking dish large enough to hold the fish and stir to combine. Add the fish and turn to coat in the mixture. Cover and place in the refrigerator to marinate for 30 minutes.

2. Meanwhile, brush four large squares of baking paper with oil.

3. Divide the beans evenly between the prepared squares of paper, piling them in the middle. Scatter the tomatoes evenly over them. Top each pile of vegetables with a fish fillet and some of the marinade. Fold up the packets securely, leaving a little room for the steam to circulate, and place them in the slow cooker. Cover and cook on high for about 2 hours, until the halibut is flaky and cooked through.

4. To serve, carefully remove the packets from the slow cooker, open them and slide the contents onto warmed plates, then garnish with spring onions, coriander and basil.

JAMBALAYA

serves **4**

½ tsp cayenne pepper

2 tsp chopped fresh thyme

350 g/12 oz skinless, boneless chicken
    breasts, diced

2 tbsp corn oil

2 onions, chopped

2 garlic cloves, finely chopped

2 green peppers, deseeded and chopped

2 celery sticks, chopped

115 g/4 oz smoked ham, chopped

175 g/6 oz chorizo sausage, sliced

400 g/14 oz canned chopped tomatoes

2 tbsp tomato purée

225 ml/8 fl oz chicken stock

450 g/1 lb raw prawns,
    peeled and deveined

450 g/1 lb cooked rice

salt and pepper

snipped fresh chives, to garnish

A great rice dish with a long history. Traditionally from Louisiana, it's also related to the Spanish national dish, paella, which uses a combination of chicken, spicy sausage and shellfish.

1. Mix together the cayenne pepper, ½ teaspoon of pepper, 1 teaspoon of salt and the thyme in a bowl. Add the chicken and toss to coat.

2. Heat the oil in a large, heavy-based saucepan. Add the onions, garlic, green peppers and celery and cook over a low heat, stirring occasionally, for 5 minutes. Add the chicken and cook over a medium heat, stirring frequently, for a further 5 minutes, until golden all over. Stir in the ham, chorizo, tomatoes, tomato purée and stock and bring to the boil.

3. Transfer the mixture to the slow cooker. Cover and cook on low for 6 hours. Add the prawns and rice, re-cover and cook on high for 30 minutes.

4. Taste and adjust the seasoning, adding salt and pepper if necessary. Transfer to warmed plates, garnish with chives and serve immediately.

SALMON WITH LEEKS & CREAM

serves **4**

vegetable oil, for oiling
2 tbsp butter
2 leeks, white and light green parts
   halved lengthways, then thinly
   sliced crossways
50 ml/2 fl oz dry white wine
125 ml/4 fl oz double cream
1 tsp salt
½ tsp pepper
4 salmon fillets, about 175 g/6 oz each
8 small fresh sage leaves

This simple salmon dish makes an elegant meal.

1. Lightly brush four large squares of baking paper with oil.

2. Heat the butter in a large frying pan over a medium–high heat, until melted and bubbling. Add the leeks and cook, stirring occasionally, for about 5 minutes, until soft.

3. Stir in the wine and bring to the boil. Cook, stirring and scraping up any sediment from the base of the pan, for a further 3 minutes, or until most of the wine has evaporated. Stir in the cream, salt and pepper and cook, stirring, for about 2 minutes, until the cream is beginning to thicken.

4. Place one salmon fillet in the centre of each prepared paper square. Top with the leek and cream mixture, then place two sage leaves on top of each portion. Fold up the packets securely, leaving a little room for the steam to circulate, then place them in the slow cooker. Cover and cook on high for about 2 hours, until the salmon is cooked through.

5. To serve, carefully remove the packets from the slow cooker, open them and slide the contents onto warmed plates. Serve immediately.

TAGLIATELLE WITH TUNA

serves **4**

200 g/7 oz dried egg tagliatelle

400 g/14 oz canned tuna steak in oil,
   drained

1 bunch spring onions, sliced

175 g/6 oz frozen peas

2 tsp hot chilli sauce

600 ml/1 pint hot chicken stock

115 g/4 oz Cheddar cheese, grated

salt and pepper

When you just want a simple and tasty meal, this is the perfect choice. Serve with some crusty bread, a crisp salad and maybe a glass of white wine.

1. Bring a large saucepan of lightly salted water to the boil. Add the pasta, return to the boil and cook for 2 minutes, until the pasta ribbons are loose. Drain.

2. Break up the tuna into bite-sized chunks and place in the slow cooker with the pasta, spring onions and peas. Season to taste with salt and pepper.

3. Add the chilli sauce to the stock and pour over the ingredients in the slow cooker. Sprinkle the grated cheese over the top. Cover and cook on low for 2 hours. Serve immediately on warmed plates.

CHAPTER 3
EASY ENTERTAINING

Chicken in Riesling 99

Mini Chicken Pot Pies 100

Chipotle Chicken Stew 103

Chicken Breasts Stuffed with Herbed Goat's Cheese 104

Turkey & Rice Casserole 107

Turkey Breast with Bacon, Leeks & Prunes 108

Sausage & Bean Cassoulet 110

Pork Stuffed with Apples 112

Ham Cooked in Cider 115

Beef Ribs Braised in Red Wine 116

Pot Roast with Beer 119

Steak Roulades with Spinach & Feta Cheese 120

Lamb Shanks with Olives 122

Honey-glazed Duck Legs 124

South-western Seafood Stew 127

Easy Bouillabaisse with Garlic Mayonnaise 128

Salmon with Dill & Lime 131

Clams in Spicy Broth with Chorizo 132

Sea Bream in Lemon Sauce 135

Halibut with Fennel & Olives 136

CHICKEN IN RIESLING

serves **4 – 6**

2 tbsp plain flour
1 chicken, weighing 1.6 kg/3 lb 8 oz,
  cut into 8 pieces
55 g/2 oz unsalted butter
1 tbsp sunflower oil
4 shallots, finely chopped
12 button mushrooms, sliced
2 tbsp brandy
500 ml/18 fl oz Riesling wine
250 ml/9 fl oz double cream
salt and pepper
cooked green vegetables,
  to serve

1. Put the flour into a polythene bag and season to taste. Add the chicken pieces, in batches, hold the top securely and shake well to coat. Transfer the chicken to a plate.

2. Heat half the butter with the oil in a heavy-based frying pan. Add the chicken pieces and cook over a medium–high heat, turning frequently, for 10 minutes, until golden all over. Using a slotted spoon, transfer them to a plate.

3. Wipe out the pan with kitchen paper, then return to a medium–high heat and melt the remaining butter. Add the shallots and mushrooms and cook, stirring constantly, for 3 minutes. Return the chicken to the frying pan and remove it from the heat. Warm the brandy in a small ladle, ignite and pour it over the chicken, shaking the pan gently until the flames have died down.

4. Return the pan to the heat and pour in the wine. Bring to the boil over a low heat, scraping up any sediment from the base of the pan. Transfer to the slow cooker, cover and cook on low for 5–6 hours, until the chicken is tender and cooked through.

5. Transfer the chicken to a serving dish and keep warm. Skim off any fat from the surface of the cooking liquid and pour the liquid into a saucepan. Stir in the cream and bring just to the boil over a low heat and pour over the chicken. Serve immediately with green vegetables.

MINI CHICKEN POT PIES

serves **6**

3 tbsp butter
1 onion, diced
115 g/4 oz button mushrooms, diced
675 g/1 lb 8 oz boneless,
    skinless chicken, diced
1 carrot, diced
2 celery sticks, diced
1 tbsp fresh thyme leaves
2 tbsp plain flour
225 ml/8 fl oz milk
175 ml/6 fl oz chicken stock
1 tsp salt
½ tsp pepper
2 sheets ready-rolled puff pastry
flour, for dusting

1. Melt 1 tablespoon of the butter in a large frying pan over a medium–high heat. Add the onion and cook, stirring, for about 5 minutes, until soft. Add the mushrooms and cook, stirring, for a further 3 minutes, or until the mushrooms are beginning to soften. Transfer the mixture to the slow cooker and add the chicken, carrot, celery and thyme.

2. Reduce the heat under the frying pan to medium, add the remaining butter and heat until melted. Whisk in the flour and cook, whisking constantly, until the mixture is lightly browned and begins to give off a nutty aroma. Whisk in the milk, stock, salt and pepper and continue to cook, stirring, for a further 5 minutes, or until the mixture begins to thicken.

3. Add the mixture to the slow cooker and stir to mix well. Cover and cook on high for about 4 hours or on low for about 8 hours, until the chicken is tender and sauce has thickened. Divide the filling equally between six 225-g/8-oz ramekins.

4. Preheat the oven to 190°C/375°F/Gas Mark 5. Roll out the pastry on a lightly floured surface and cut out six rounds, each about 2.5 cm/1 inch larger in circumference than the ramekins. Top each filled ramekin with a pastry round, crimping the edges. Prick the pastry on each pie several times with a fork.

5. Place the ramekins on a baking sheet and bake in the preheated oven for about 20 minutes, until the pastry is puffed and golden brown. Leave to cool for about 10 minutes before serving.

CHIPOTLE CHICKEN STEW

serves **4 – 6**

200 g/7 oz dried haricot beans,
   soaked overnight
1 large onion, sliced
1 dried chipotle pepper, soaked for
   20 minutes, then drained and
   finely chopped
1.5 kg/3 lb 5 oz oven-ready chicken
200 ml/7 fl oz hot chicken stock
400 g/14 oz canned chopped tomatoes
1 tsp ground cumin
salt and pepper

It couldn't be any easier to create a great-tasting meal. Just cook some rice or pasta, toss some salad leaves in a bowl and you're ready to serve.

1. Drain and rinse the beans and place in a saucepan, cover with cold water and bring to the boil. Boil rapidly for 10 minutes, then remove from the heat and drain and rinse again.

2. Transfer the beans to the slow cooker and add the onion and chipotle pepper. Place the chicken on top, pour over the stock and tomatoes with their can juices, sprinkle with cumin and season to taste with salt and pepper.

3. Cover and cook for 4 hours on high. Carefully remove the chicken and cut into eight pieces. Skim the excess fat from the juices and adjust the seasoning.

4. Spoon the beans into a warmed serving dish, top with the chicken and spoon the juices over. Serve immediately.

CHICKEN BREASTS STUFFED WITH HERBED GOAT'S CHEESE

serves **4**

225 g/8 oz soft, fresh goat's cheese

10 g/¼ oz fresh basil leaves,
   finely chopped

2 spring onions, thinly sliced

2 garlic cloves, finely chopped

4 boneless, skinless chicken breasts

2 tbsp olive oil

200 g/7 oz chard, central ribs removed,
   cut into wide ribbons

225 ml/8 fl oz dry white wine,
   chicken stock or water

salt and pepper

Filling chicken breasts with herb-studded goat's cheese turns them into sophisticated dinner party fare.

1. Put the cheese, basil, spring onions and garlic into a mixing bowl and stir to combine.

2. Lay the chicken breasts flat on a chopping board. Working with one breast at a time, place your hand on top of the breast and press down to keep it in place. With the other hand, using a large, sharp cook's knife, slice the breast horizontally, leaving one edge intact like a hinge.

3. Open the butterflied breasts and spoon equal amounts of the cheese mixture onto one half of each. Fold closed and secure with wooden cocktail sticks or kitchen string. Season the breasts with salt and pepper.

4. Heat the oil in a large frying pan over a medium–high heat until very hot, then add the chicken. Cook on one side for 4 minutes, until brown, then turn and cook on the other side for a further 4 minutes, until brown.

5. Put the chard and the wine into the slow cooker. Arrange the stuffed chicken breasts on top of the chard, cover and cook on high for about 2 hours or on low for about 4 hours, until the chicken is cooked through. Serve hot.

TURKEY & RICE CASSEROLE

serves **4**

1 tbsp olive oil

500 g/1 lb 2 oz turkey breast, diced

1 onion, diced

2 carrots, diced

2 celery sticks, sliced

250 g/9 oz closed-cup mushrooms, sliced

175 g/6 oz long-grain rice,
   preferably Basmati

450 ml/16 fl oz hot chicken stock

salt and pepper

A great low-fat recipe if you're counting the calories, and turkey makes a change from chicken too. Serve with soy or chilli sauce to accompany.

1. Heat the oil in a heavy-based frying pan, add the turkey and fry over a high heat for 3–4 minutes, until lightly browned.

2. Combine the onion, carrots, celery, mushrooms and rice in the slow cooker. Arrange the turkey on top, season well with salt and pepper and pour the stock over. Cover and cook on high for 2 hours.

3. Stir lightly with a fork to mix, adjust the seasoning to taste and serve immediately.

TURKEY BREAST WITH BACON, LEEKS & PRUNES

serves **6 – 8**

115 g/4 oz bacon rashers

2 leeks, trimmed, white and light green
    parts, thinly sliced

1 skinless, bone-in turkey breast
    (about 1.8 kg/4 lb)

30 g/1 oz plain flour

1 tbsp olive oil, if needed

12 stoned prunes, halved
    (quartered, if large)

1 tsp crumbled dried thyme or 1 tbsp
    finely chopped fresh thyme

225 ml/8 fl oz chicken stock

salt and pepper

When a whole turkey is too much, this elegant dish using just turkey breast is perfect.

1. Heat a frying pan over a medium–high heat, then add the bacon and cook until just crisp. Remove from the pan, drain on kitchen paper, then chop or crumble into small pieces.

2. Add the leeks to the pan and cook in the bacon fat over a medium–high heat, stirring frequently, for about 5 minutes, or until soft.

3. Season the turkey with salt and pepper and dredge with the flour. If needed, add the oil to the pan, then add the turkey and cook on one side for 4–5 minutes, until brown. Turn and cook on the other side for a further 4–5 minutes, until brown.

4. Place the turkey in the slow cooker together with the leeks, bacon, prunes and thyme. Add the stock, cover and cook on high for about 5 hours or on low for about 9 hours.

5. Remove the turkey from the slow cooker and leave to rest for 5 minutes. Slice and serve with some of the sauce, including the prunes and bits of bacon, spooned over the top.

SAUSAGE & BEAN CASSOULET

serves **4**

2 tbsp sunflower oil
2 onions, chopped
2 garlic cloves, finely chopped
115 g/4 oz streaky bacon, chopped
500 g/1 lb 2 oz pork sausages
400 g/14 oz canned haricot, red kidney
    or black-eyed beans, drained and
    rinsed
2 tbsp chopped fresh parsley
150 ml/5 fl oz hot beef stock

To serve
4 slices French bread
55 g/2 oz Gruyère cheese, grated

Slow cooking at its best. Here is a variation on the famous regional French casserole, named after the pot it's traditionally cooked in. Use good quality sausages for the best result.

1. Heat the oil in a heavy-based frying pan. Add the onions and cook over a low heat, stirring occasionally, for 5 minutes, until softened. Add the garlic, bacon and sausages and cook, stirring and turning the sausages occasionally, for a further 5 minutes.

2. Using a slotted spoon, transfer the mixture from the frying pan to the slow cooker. Add the beans, parsley and stock, then cover and cook on low for 6 hours.

3. Shortly before serving, preheat the grill. Place the bread slices on the grill rack and lightly toast on one side under the preheated grill. Turn the slices over, sprinkle with the grated cheese and place under the grill until just melted.

4. Serve the cassoulet and the bread slices immediately.

PORK STUFFED WITH APPLES

serves **4**

1 large apple, peeled and sliced
125 ml/4 fl oz apple juice or water
4 boneless pork chops,
    about 2.5 cm/1 inch thick
4 slices prosciutto
115 g/4 oz Gorgonzola cheese
salt and pepper
mashed potato, to serve

A great taste combination with sweet apples, salty ham and pungent Gorgonzola to offset the natural richness of the pork.

1. Place half of the apple slices in the base of the slow cooker and add the apple juice.

2. Butterfly the pork chops by laying each chop flat on a chopping board and, pressing down on it with the flat of your hand to keep it in place, cutting through the centre horizontally, leaving one side attached like a hinge. Loosely wrap in clingfilm and gently pound with a meat mallet to a thickness of about 2 cm/¾ inch.

3. Open the flattened and butterflied chops like books and place on the chopping board. Layer each chop with a slice of prosciutto, a quarter of the cheese and a quarter of the remaining apple slices. Fold closed and secure with wooden cocktail sticks.

4. Season the stuffed chops all over with salt and pepper and place in the slow cooker on top of the apple slices. Cover and cook on high for about 4 hours or on low for about 7 hours, until the meat is cooked through. Serve hot with mashed potato.

HAM COOKED IN CIDER

serves **6**

1 kg/2 lb 4 oz boneless gammon joint
1 onion, halved
4 cloves
6 black peppercorns
1 tsp juniper berries
1 celery stick, chopped
1 carrot, sliced
1 litre/1¾ pints medium cider
fresh salad, to serve

A gammon joint makes a great mid-week roast and cooking it this way ensures the meat stays moist. Any cold leftovers will make excellent sandwiches.

1. Place a trivet or rack in the slow cooker, if you like, and stand the gammon on it. Otherwise, just place the gammon in the slow cooker. Stud each onion half with two of the cloves and add to the slow cooker with the peppercorns, juniper berries, celery and carrot.

2. Pour in the cider, cover and cook on low for 8 hours, until the meat is tender.

3. Remove the gammon from the cooker and place on a board. Tent with foil and leave to stand for 10–15 minutes. Discard the cooking liquid and flavourings.

4. Cut off any rind and fat from the gammon joint and carve into slices. Transfer to serving plates and serve immediately with a fresh salad.

BEEF RIBS BRAISED IN RED WINE

serves **6**

1.3 kg/3 lb bone-in beef short ribs

2 tbsp vegetable oil, plus extra, if needed

1 onion, diced

1 celery stick, diced

1 carrot, diced

1 tbsp tomato purée

3 fresh thyme sprigs

2 garlic cloves, finely chopped

3 tbsp plain flour

450 ml/16 fl oz red wine

225 ml/8 fl oz beef stock

1 bay leaf

salt and pepper

mashed potato or cooked polenta,
  to serve

If possible, ask your butcher to cut the ribs into thirds for easier serving.

1. Generously season the ribs with salt and pepper. Heat the oil in a large, heavy-based frying pan over a medium–high heat. Add the ribs and cook, turning occasionally, for about 10 minutes, until brown on all sides. Transfer to the slow cooker.

2. Add more oil to the pan if needed and, when hot, add the onion, celery and carrot to the pan. Cook, stirring occasionally, for about 15 minutes, until the vegetables are soft. Add the tomato purée, thyme, garlic and flour and cook, stirring, for a further 1 minute.

3. Add the wine, bring to the boil and cook for a further 1–2 minutes, stirring and scraping up any sediment from the base of the pan. Reduce the heat to medium–low and simmer for 6–8 minutes, until the liquid is reduced by about half. Transfer to the slow cooker.

4. Stir in the stock, ½ teaspoon of salt and the bay leaf, cover and cook on high for 7 hours or on low for 10 hours, until the meat is very tender and falling from the bone. About 1–2 hours before the end of cooking, set the lid ajar, if desired, to allow the liquid to reduce and reach a thicker consistency.

5. Before serving, remove and discard the thyme and bay leaf. Serve hot with the mashed potato.

POT ROAST WITH BEER

serves **4 – 6**

2 small onions, each cut into
  8 wedges
8 small carrots, halved lengthways
1 fennel bulb, cut into 8 wedges
2.25 kg/5 lb rolled chuck steak
2 tbsp Dijon mustard
1 tbsp plain flour
100 ml/3½ fl oz beer
salt and pepper

*There are many great beers that you can try
in this recipe, although the darker ones will
give the best flavour. Serve accompanied by
buttery mashed potatoes.*

1. Place the onions, carrots and fennel in the slow cooker and
season to taste with salt and pepper. Place the beef on top.

2. Mix the mustard and flour together to form a paste and
spread it over the beef. Season well and pour over the beer.
Cover and cook on low for 8 hours.

3. Remove the beef and vegetables with a slotted spoon and
transfer to a warmed serving platter. Skim the excess fat from
the juices and pour the juices into a jug to serve with the beef.
Serve immediately.

STEAK ROULADES WITH SPINACH & FETA CHEESE

serves **4**

4 chuck steaks, about 675 g/
  1 lb 8 oz in total, pounded to a
  thickness of 1 cm/½ inch
½ onion, diced
115 g/4 oz feta cheese, crumbled
30 g/1 oz stoned Kalamata olives,
  chopped
4 small handfuls baby spinach leaves
50 ml/2 fl oz beef stock or water
salt and pepper

Rolling steak around a flavoursome filling makes for an elegant presentation of a surprisingly simple dish.

1. Season the steaks on both sides with salt and pepper. Top each steak with a quarter each of the onion, cheese, olives and spinach. Starting with one of the short sides, roll up the steaks into pinwheels and secure with kitchen string or wooden cocktail sticks.

2. Place the steak rolls in the slow cooker along with the stock, cover, and cook on high for about 3 hours or on low for 6 hours, until the meat is tender and cooked through. Serve hot.

LAMB SHANKS WITH OLIVES

serves **4**

1½ tbsp plain flour
4 lamb shanks
2 tbsp olive oil
1 onion, sliced
2 garlic cloves, finely chopped
2 tsp sweet paprika
400 g/14 oz canned chopped tomatoes
2 tbsp tomato purée
2 carrots, sliced
2 tsp sugar
225 ml/8 fl oz red wine
5-cm/2-inch cinnamon stick
2 fresh rosemary sprigs
115 g/4 oz stoned black olives
2 tbsp lemon juice
2 tbsp chopped fresh mint,
   plus extra leaves to garnish
salt and pepper

1. Put the flour into a polythene bag and season to taste with salt and pepper. Add the lamb shanks, hold the top securely and shake well to coat.

2. Heat the oil in a large, heavy-based saucepan. Add the lamb shanks and cook over a medium heat, turning frequently, for 6–8 minutes, until evenly browned. Transfer to a plate and set aside.

3. Add the onion and garlic to the saucepan and cook, stirring frequently, for 5 minutes, until softened. Stir in the paprika and cook for 1 minute. Add the tomatoes, tomato purée, carrots, sugar, wine, cinnamon stick and rosemary and bring to the boil.

4. Transfer the mixture to the slow cooker and add the lamb shanks. Cover and cook on low for 8 hours, until the lamb is very tender.

5. Add the olives, lemon juice and chopped mint to the slow cooker. Re-cover and cook on high for 30 minutes. Remove and discard the rosemary and cinnamon stick. Transfer to warmed serving plates, garnish with mint leaves and serve immediately.

HONEY-GLAZED DUCK LEGS

serves **4 – 6**

6 duck legs
125 ml/4 fl oz chicken stock
3 tbsp red wine or white wine
115 g/4 oz clear honey
1 tbsp fresh thyme leaves
salt and pepper
mashed potato or cooked polenta,
  to serve

This elegant alternative to chicken legs is a great dinner party dish.

1. Trim any excess skin or fat from the duck legs and season with salt and pepper. Heat a large, heavy-based frying pan over a medium–high heat. When the pan is very hot, add the duck legs, in batches, if necessary, and cook on one side for about 4 minutes, until brown. Turn and cook on the other side for about 4 minutes, until brown. Transfer to the slow cooker.

2. Put the stock, wine, honey and thyme into a small bowl, stir to combine, then pour the mixture over the duck legs, turning to coat. Cover and cook on high for about 6 hours or on low for about 10 hours, until the duck is very tender. Serve hot with mashed potato or polenta.

SOUTH-WESTERN SEAFOOD STEW

serves **4**

2 tbsp olive oil, plus extra for drizzling
1 large onion, chopped
4 garlic cloves, finely chopped
1 yellow pepper, deseeded and chopped
1 red pepper, deseeded and chopped
1 orange pepper, deseeded and chopped
450 g/1 lb tomatoes, peeled and chopped
2 large mild green chillies,
   such as poblano, chopped
finely grated rind and juice of 1 lime
2 tbsp chopped fresh coriander,
   plus extra leaves to garnish
1 bay leaf
450 ml/16 fl oz fish, vegetable or
   chicken stock
450 g/1 lb red mullet fillets
450 g/1 lb raw prawns
225 g/8 oz prepared squid
salt and pepper

The flavours of lime and fresh coriander leaves give this healthy yet hearty fish stew a rich flavour.

1. Heat the oil in a saucepan. Add the onion and garlic and cook over a low heat, stirring occasionally, for 5 minutes, until softened. Add the peppers, tomatoes and chillies and cook, stirring frequently, for 5 minutes. Stir in the lime rind and juice, add the chopped coriander and bay leaf and pour in the stock. Bring to the boil, stirring occasionally.

2. Transfer the mixture to the slow cooker, cover and cook on low for 7½ hours. Meanwhile, skin the fish fillets, if necessary, and cut the flesh into chunks. Peel and devein the prawns. Cut the squid bodies into rings and halve the tentacles or leave them whole.

3. Add the seafood to the stew, season to taste with salt and pepper, re-cover and cook on high for 30 minutes, or until tender and cooked through. Remove and discard the bay leaf. Transfer to warmed serving bowls, garnish with coriander leaves and serve immediately.

EASY BOUILLABAISSE WITH GARLIC MAYONNAISE

serves **4**

pinch of saffron threads
1 tbsp hot water
2 tbsp olive oil
1 onion, diced
3 garlic cloves, finely chopped
2 celery sticks, finely chopped
2 tsp crumbled, dried oregano
1 tsp salt
¼–½ tsp crushed dried red pepper flakes
350 ml/12 fl oz dry white wine
400 g/14 oz canned tomato purée
400 g/14 oz canned chopped tomatoes,
    with juice
12 small clams, scrubbed
12 mussels, scrubbed and debearded
450 g/1 lb white fish fillet, such as
    halibut, cut into 5-cm/2-inch pieces
225 g/8 oz raw prawns,
    peeled and deveined
2 tbsp finely chopped fresh parsley,
    to garnish

Garlic mayonnaise
2 garlic cloves, finely chopped
½ tsp salt
125 ml/4 fl oz mayonnaise

This simplified version of the French classic is sure to impress. Feel free to add or substitute other types of fish or shellfish.

1. Place the saffron in a small bowl and cover with the hot water. Heat the oil in a large frying pan over a medium–high heat. Add the onion and garlic and cook, stirring, for about 5 minutes, until soft. Add the celery, oregano, salt and red pepper flakes, then add the wine. Bring to the boil and cook, stirring, for about 8 minutes, until the liquid is reduced by half. Transfer the mixture to the slow cooker.

2. Stir in the saffron and its soaking water, tomato purée and tomatoes with their can juices. Cover and cook on high for about 2 hours or on low for about 4 hours.

3. Discard any clams or mussels with broken shells and any that refuse to close when tapped. Add the fish, prawns, clams and mussels, cover and cook on high for a further 10–15 minutes, until the fish and prawns are cooked through and the clams and mussels have opened, discarding any that still remain closed.

4. To make the garlic mayonnaise, mash the garlic and salt together with a fork to make a paste. Stir in the mayonnaise. To serve, ladle some broth into four serving bowls, then add some of the fish and shellfish. Top each serving with a dollop of the garlic mayonnaise, garnish with parsley and serve immediately.

SALMON WITH DILL & LIME

serves **4**

40 g/1½ oz butter, melted

1 onion, thinly sliced

450 g/1 lb potatoes, thinly sliced

100 ml/3½ fl oz hot fish stock or water

4 pieces skinless salmon fillet,
    about 140 g/5 oz each

juice of 1 lime

2 tbsp chopped fresh dill

salt and pepper

lime wedges, to serve

The delicate flavour of salmon is retained in this simply cooked fish dish. Serve with tender French beans or peas for an elegant lunch or dinner.

1. Brush the base of the slow cooker with 1 tablespoon of the butter. Layer the onion and potatoes in the dish, sprinkling with salt and pepper between the layers. Add the stock and drizzle with 1 tablespoon of the butter. Cover and cook on low for 3 hours.

2. Arrange the salmon over the vegetables in a single layer. Drizzle the lime juice over, sprinkle with dill and salt and pepper and pour the remaining butter on top. Cover and cook on low for a further 1 hour, until the fish flakes easily.

3. Serve the salmon and vegetables on warmed plates with the juices spooned over and lime wedges on the side.

CLAMS IN SPICY BROTH WITH CHORIZO

serves **4**

1 tbsp olive oil

1 red onion, halved lengthways
 and sliced

115 g/4 oz chorizo sausage, diced

1 fennel bulb, coarsely chopped

400 g/14 oz canned chopped tomatoes,
 with juice

125 ml/4 fl oz dry white wine

125 ml/4 fl oz clam juice or water

½ tsp salt

¼–½ tsp crushed red pepper flakes

900 g/2 lb small clams, scrubbed

2 tbsp chopped fresh flat-leaf parsley,
 to garnish

green salad and crusty bread, to serve

This festive, yet simple shellfish dish makes a lovely light meal served with a crisp green salad and plenty of fresh crusty bread for soaking up the delicious broth.

1. Heat the oil in a large frying pan over a medium–high heat. Add the onion and cook, stirring, for about 5 minutes, until soft. Add the chorizo and continue to cook, stirring occasionally, until the meat begins to brown. Transfer the mixture to the slow cooker.

2. Stir in the fennel, tomatoes and their can juices, wine, clam juice, salt and red pepper flakes. Cover and cook on high for about 2 hours or on low for about 4 hours.

3. Discard any clams with broken shells and any that refuse to close when tapped. Add the clams to the slow cooker, cover and cook on high for a further 10–15 minutes, until the clams have opened. Discard any clams that remain closed.

4. Serve the clams in bowls, with a generous amount of broth, garnished with parsley and accompanied by a green salad and crusty bread.

SEA BREAM IN LEMON SAUCE

serves **4**

8 sea bream fillets
55 g/2 oz unsalted butter
25 g/1 oz plain flour
850 ml/1½ pints warm milk
4 tbsp lemon juice
225 g/8 oz mushrooms, sliced
1 bouquet garni
salt and pepper
lemon wedges and griddled asparagus,
   to serve

Use red snapper or sea bass if bream is not available for this simple yet delicious fish dish with a lemon flavoured mushroom sauce.

1. Put the fish fillets into the slow cooker and set aside.

2. Melt the butter in a saucepan over a low heat. Add the flour and cook, stirring constantly, for 1 minute. Gradually stir in the milk, a little at a time, and bring to the boil, stirring constantly. Stir in the lemon juice and mushrooms, add the bouquet garni and season to taste with salt and pepper. Reduce the heat and simmer for 5 minutes. Pour the sauce over the fish fillets, cover and cook on low for 1½ hours.

3. Carefully lift out the fish fillets and transfer to warmed serving plates. Serve immediately with lemon wedges and griddled asparagus.

HALIBUT WITH FENNEL & OLIVES

serves **4**

vegetable oil, for brushing
2 tbsp olive oil
50 g/1¾ oz stoned Kalamata olives,
  chopped
1 garlic clove, finely chopped
1 small shallot, finely chopped
zest of 1 lemon
1 tbsp finely chopped fresh oregano
1 fennel bulb, thinly sliced
4 halibut fillets, about 175 g/6 oz each
50 ml/2 fl oz dry white wine
cooked couscous, to serve

Fresh fennel adds a unique flavour to this simple halibut dish.

1. Lightly brush four 30 x 30-cm/12 x 12-inch squares of baking paper with vegetable oil.

2. Put the olive oil, olives, garlic, shallot, lemon zest and oregano into a bowl and mix to combine.

3. Pile equal amounts of the fennel slices in the middle of the prepared squares of baking paper. Top each pile of fennel with a halibut fillet. Spoon the olive mixture over the fish.

4. Drizzle the wine over the fish. Fold up the packets, leaving a little room for steam circulation, and place them in the slow cooker. Cover and cook on high for about 2 hours, until the fish is cooked through.

5. To serve, open up the packets and gently transfer the contents to warmed plates. Serve immediately with couscous.

CHAPTER 4
VEGETARIAN

Baked Eggs with Caramelized Onions & Cheese 140

Winter Vegetable Medley 142

Vegetable Pasta 145

Louisiana Courgettes 146

Butternut Squash & Goat's Cheese Enchiladas 148

Summer Vegetable Casserole 151

Wild Mushroom Lasagne 152

Parsley Dumpling Stew 155

Pumpkin Risotto 156

Vegetable Curry 159

Indian-spiced Chickpeas 160

Baked Aubergine with Courgette 163

Tofu with Spicy Peanut Sauce 164

Mixed Bean Chilli 167

Stuffed Butternut Squash 168

Macaroni Cheese with Toasted Breadcrumbs 170

White Bean Stew 172

Vegetarian Paella 175

Spaghetti with Lentil Bolognese Sauce 176

Asparagus & Spinach Risotto 179

BAKED EGGS WITH CARAMELIZED ONIONS & CHEESE

serves **4**

4 tbsp butter, plus extra for greasing
1 onion, halved and thinly sliced
4 tbsp double cream
55 g/2 oz freshly grated vegetarian
    Parmesan-style cheese
4 large eggs
8 small fresh sage leaves
salt and pepper

Perfectly cooked eggs served in a rich, creamy sauce make a beautiful brunch dish or a sophisticated first course.

1. Grease four 175-g/6-oz ramekins with butter. Fill the slow cooker with hot water to a depth of 2.5 cm/1 inch, cover and turn on to high.

2. Melt the butter in a large frying pan over a medium–high heat. Add the onions and cook, stirring occasionally, for about 6 minutes, until soft and just beginning to brown. Reduce the heat to medium, add 3 tablespoons of the cream and continue to cook, stirring occasionally, for a further 5 minutes, or until the cream is beginning to thicken.

3. Stir in the cheese. Season the mixture to taste with salt and pepper and divide between the prepared ramekins.

4. Break an egg into each ramekin, season with a little more salt and pepper, then top each egg with two sage leaves and evenly drizzle the remaining cream over the eggs.

5. Cover each ramekin with foil and place carefully in the water bath in the slow cooker. Cover the slow cooker and cook on high for about 1 hour, until the eggs are set to your liking. Serve hot in the ramekins.

WINTER VEGETABLE MEDLEY

serves **4**

2 tbsp sunflower oil
2 onions, chopped
3 carrots, chopped
3 parsnips, chopped
2 bunches celery, chopped
2 tbsp chopped fresh parsley
1 tbsp chopped fresh coriander
300 ml/10 fl oz vegetable stock
salt and pepper

Serve this herb-flavoured vegetable stew with brown rice or pasta for a tasty and nutritious meal. Toasted seeds or nuts sprinkled on top will give crunch.

1. Heat the oil in a large, heavy-based saucepan. Add the onions and cook over a medium heat, stirring occasionally, for 5 minutes until softened. Add the carrots, parsnips and celery and cook, stirring occasionally, for a further 5 minutes. Stir in the herbs, season with salt and pepper and pour in the stock. Bring to the boil.

2. Transfer the vegetable mixture to the slow cooker, cover and cook on high for 3 hours until tender. Taste and adjust the seasoning if necessary. Using a slotted spoon, transfer the medley to warmed plates, then spoon over a little of the cooking liquid. Serve immediately.

VEGETABLE PASTA

serves **4**

250 g/9 oz dried penne pasta
2 tbsp olive oil, plus extra for drizzling
1 red onion, sliced
2 courgettes, thinly sliced
200 g/7 oz closed cup mushrooms, sliced
2 tbsp chopped fresh oregano
300 g/10½ oz tomatoes, sliced
55 g/2 oz freshly grated vegetarian
   Parmesan-style cheese
salt and pepper

Layers of pasta and sliced vegetables with a sprinkling of fresh herbs and vegetarian cheese make a satisfying meal for any occasion.

1. Bring a large pan of lightly salted water to the boil. Add the pasta, bring back to the boil and cook for 8–10 minutes, or until tender but still firm to the bite. Drain. Meanwhile, heat the oil in a heavy-based saucepan, add the onion and cook over a medium heat, stirring occasionally, for 5 minutes, until softened. Stir into the pasta.

2. Place a layer of courgettes and mushrooms in the slow cooker and top with layer of pasta. Sprinkle with oregano, salt and pepper and continue layering, finishing with a layer of vegetables.

3. Arrange the sliced tomatoes on top and drizzle with oil. Cover and cook on high for 3 hours, or until tender.

4. Sprinkle with cheese, cover and cook for a further 10 minutes. Transfer to a warmed serving bowl and serve immediately.

LOUISIANA COURGETTES

serves **6**

1 kg/2 lb 4 oz courgettes, thickly sliced
1 onion, finely chopped
2 garlic cloves, finely chopped
2 red peppers, deseeded and chopped
5 tbsp hot vegetable stock
4 tomatoes, peeled and chopped
25 g/1 oz butter, diced
salt and cayenne pepper
crusty bread, to serve

Use a mixture of green and yellow courgettes for added colour in this simple vegetable recipe. It can be served as a side dish for non-vegetarians.

1. Place the courgettes, onion, garlic and red peppers in the slow cooker and season to taste with salt and cayenne pepper. Pour in the stock and mix well.

2. Sprinkle the chopped tomatoes on top and dot with the butter. Cover and cook on high for 2½ hours until tender. Serve immediately with crusty bread.

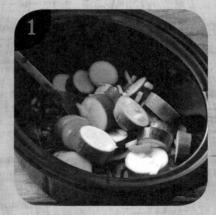

BUTTERNUT SQUASH & GOAT'S CHEESE ENCHILADAS

serves **4**

1 large butternut squash,
   peeled and diced
4 tbsp olive oil
1 tsp salt
3 tsp ground cumin
1 large onion, diced
3 garlic cloves, finely chopped
1 tbsp hot or mild chilli powder
1 tbsp dried oregano
450g/1 lb canned puréed tomatoes
   or passata
1 tbsp clear honey
450 ml/16 fl oz vegetable stock
12 corn tortillas
225 g/8 oz soft, fresh goat's cheese

Roasting butternut squash caramelizes it, giving an enticing sweetness that balances out the spicy sauce and salty cheese.

1. Preheat the oven to 200°C/400°F/Gas Mark 6. Line a baking tray with baking paper. Coat the squash with 2 tablespoons of the oil, sprinkle with half the salt and 1 teaspoon of the cumin. Place the squash on the tray and roast for 30–40 minutes, until soft and beginning to brown.

2. Heat the remaining oil in a large frying pan over a medium–high heat. Add the onion and garlic and cook, stirring, for about 5 minutes, until soft. Add the remaining cumin and salt, the chilli powder and the oregano and cook for a further 1 minute. Stir in the puréed tomatoes, honey and stock, bring to the boil and cook for about 5 minutes. Purée the sauce in a food processor or blender.

3. Coat the base of the slow cooker with a little sauce. Make a layer of tortillas, tearing them if necessary, to cover the bottom of the slow cooker. Top the tortillas with a layer of the squash, a layer of cheese, a layer of sauce, then another layer of tortillas.

4. Layer again with squash, cheese and sauce. Finish with a layer of tortillas, sauce and the remaining cheese. Cover and cook on low for 2 hours, until the tortillas are soft and the cheese is melted and bubbling. Serve hot.

SUMMER VEGETABLE CASSEROLE

serves **4**

500 g/1 lb 2 oz potatoes,
   cubed
2 courgettes, cubed
2 red peppers, deseeded and cubed
2 red onions, sliced
2 tsp mixed dried herbs
250 ml/9 fl oz hot vegetable stock
salt and pepper

As an alternative, use sliced baby new potatoes with the skin left on for extra nutritional value. You can add other summer vegetables that are available to vary the recipe.

1. Layer all the vegetables in the slow cooker, sprinkling with herbs and salt and pepper between the layers.

2. Pour over the stock. Cover and cook on low for 7 hours. Transfer to warmed serving bowls and serve immediately.

WILD MUSHROOM LASAGNE

serves **4 – 6**

vegetable oil, for brushing
225 g/8 oz lasagne sheets
25 g/1 oz freshly grated vegetarian
   Parmesan-style cheese

Filling
25 g/1 oz dried ceps
450 ml/16 fl oz boiling water
2 tbsp olive oil
1 small onion, diced
2 garlic cloves, finely chopped
450 g/1 lb button mushrooms or
   chestnut mushrooms, sliced
125 ml/4 fl oz red wine
1 tbsp finely chopped fresh thyme leaves
½ tsp salt
½ tsp pepper

Sauce
55 g/2 oz unsalted butter
35 g/1¼ oz plain flour
600 ml/1 pint milk
85 g/3 oz freshly grated vegetarian
   Parmesan-style cheese
¾ tsp salt

1. To make the filling, soak the ceps in the water for 30 minutes. Remove the mushrooms, reserving the liquid, and chop. Heat the oil in a large frying pan over a medium–high heat. Add the onion and garlic and cook, stirring, for 5 minutes. Add the fresh and reconstituted mushrooms and cook, stirring, for about 5 minutes, until soft. Add the wine, bring to the boil and cook for about 5 minutes, until the liquid has almost evaporated. Add the mushroom soaking liquid, thyme, salt and pepper and cook over a medium–high heat, stirring frequently, for a further 5 minutes, or until the liquid is reduced by half.

2. To make the sauce, melt the butter in a large saucepan over a medium heat. Whisk in the flour and cook, whisking constantly, for about 3 minutes, until the mixture is golden brown. Whisk in the milk and bring to the boil. Reduce the heat and simmer for 3 minutes, then remove from the heat and stir in the cheese and salt.

3. To assemble the lasagne, line the slow cooker with foil, overlapping two large pieces to cover the entire base. Lightly brush the foil with oil. Spoon a thin layer of sauce and a thin layer of mushrooms over the base. Top with a layer of pasta. Repeat, to make a total of three layers. Top with a final layer of pasta, then a layer of sauce. Sprinkle the cheese over the top. Cover and cook on low for about 4 hours, until the pasta is tender and the top is brown and bubbling. Serve the lasagne directly from the slow cooker or use the foil as a sling to lift it out to serve.

PARSLEY DUMPLING STEW

serves **6**

½ swede, cut into chunks
2 onions, sliced
2 potatoes, cut into chunks
2 carrots, cut into chunks
2 celery sticks, sliced
2 courgettes, sliced
2 tbsp tomato purée
600 ml/1 pint hot vegetable stock
1 bay leaf
1 tsp ground coriander
½ tsp dried thyme
400 g/14 oz canned sweetcorn, drained
salt and pepper

Parsley dumplings
200 g/7 oz self-raising flour
pinch of salt
115 g/4 oz vegetable suet
2 tbsp chopped fresh flat-leaf parsley,
    plus extra sprigs to garnish
about 125 ml/4 fl oz milk

Non-vegetarians won't miss the meat in this vegetable stew if they have light and fluffy herb dumplings on their plates.

1. Put the swede, onions, potatoes, carrots, celery and courgettes into the slow cooker. Stir the tomato purée into the stock and pour it over the vegetables. Add the bay leaf, coriander and thyme and season to taste with salt and pepper. Cover and cook on low for 6 hours.

2. To make the dumplings, sift the flour with the salt into a bowl and stir in the suet and chopped parsley. Add just enough of the milk to make a firm but light dough. Knead lightly and shape into 12 small balls.

3. Stir the sweetcorn into the mixture in the slow cooker and place the dumplings on top. Cook on high for 30 minutes. Transfer to warmed serving plates, garnish with parsley sprigs and serve immediately.

PUMPKIN RISOTTO

serves **4**

2 tbsp olive oil
1 shallot, finely chopped
1 garlic clove, finely chopped
280 g/10 oz arborio rice
125 ml/4 fl oz dry white wine
1.2 litres/2 pints vegetable stock
425 g/15 oz canned pumpkin purée
1 tbsp finely chopped fresh sage
½ tsp salt
¼ tsp pepper
pinch of nutmeg
2 tbsp butter
115 g/4 oz freshly grated vegetarian
   Parmesan-style cheese, plus extra
   to serve

This stunning risotto, enriched with nutritious and delicious pumpkin, is a satisfying vegetarian main course for a festive autumn meal.

1. Heat the oil in a large frying pan over a medium–high heat. Add the shallot and garlic and cook, stirring, for about 5 minutes, until soft. Add the rice and cook, stirring, for 1 minute. Add the wine and cook for a further 3 minutes, until the liquid is absorbed. Transfer the mixture to the slow cooker.

2. Stir in the stock, pumpkin purée, sage, salt, pepper and nutmeg. Cover and cook on high for about 1½ hours, until the rice is tender. Stir in the butter, re-cover and cook for a further 15 minutes. Stir in the cheese and serve immediately, with a little more cheese sprinkled over.

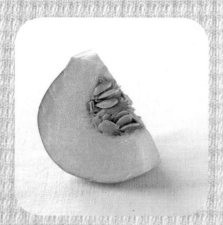

VEGETABLE CURRY

serves **4 – 6**

2 tbsp vegetable oil
1 tsp cumin seeds
1 onion, sliced
2 curry leaves
2.5-cm/1-inch piece fresh ginger,
   finely chopped
2 fresh red chillies, deseeded
   and chopped
2 tbsp Indian curry paste
2 carrots, sliced
115 g/4 oz mangetout
1 cauliflower, cut into florets
3 tomatoes, peeled and chopped
85 g/3 oz frozen peas, thawed
½ tsp ground turmeric
150–225 ml/5–8 fl oz hot vegetable stock
salt and pepper
naan breads, to serve

Every cook should have a great vegetable curry recipe and this could be the one. For non-vegetarians, it could also be served as an accompaniment to a meat or chicken curry.

1. Heat the oil in a large heavy-based saucepan. Add the cumin seeds and cook, stirring constantly, for 1–2 minutes, until they give off their aroma and begin to pop. Add the onion and curry leaves and cook, stirring occasionally, for 5 minutes, until the onion has softened. Add the ginger and chillies and cook, stirring occasionally, for 1 minute.

2. Stir in the curry paste and cook, stirring, for 2 minutes, then add the carrots, mangetout and cauliflower. Cook for 5 minutes, then add the tomatoes, peas and turmeric and season to taste with salt and pepper. Cook for 3 minutes, then add 150 ml/ 5 fl oz of the stock and bring to the boil.

3. Transfer the mixture to the slow cooker. If the vegetables are not covered by the liquid, add more hot stock, then cover and cook on low for 5 hours, until tender. Remove and discard the curry leaves. Transfer to warmed serving dishes and serve immediately with naan breads.

INDIAN-SPICED CHICKPEAS

serves **4**

2 tbsp vegetable oil
1 onion, finely chopped
2 garlic cloves, finely chopped
1 tsp ground cumin
1 tsp ground turmeric
1 tsp ground ginger
$\frac{1}{4}$–$\frac{1}{2}$ tsp cayenne pepper
350 ml/12 fl oz water
800 g/1 lb 14 oz canned chickpeas, rinsed and drained
1 tsp salt
$\frac{1}{2}$ tsp garam masala

To serve
steamed rice
yoghurt and cucumber salad

For a healthy and delicious meal, serve these spicy chickpeas with steamed rice, and a cooling yoghurt and cucumber salad.

1. Heat the oil in a large frying pan over a medium–high heat. Add the onion and garlic and cook, stirring, for about 5 minutes, until soft. Add the cumin, turmeric, ginger and cayenne pepper and cook, stirring, for a further 1 minute. Add the water and cook for a further 1–2 minutes, scraping up any sediment from the base of the pan. Transfer the mixture to the slow cooker.

2. Stir in the chickpeas, cover and cook on low for about 6 hours.

3. Just before serving, add the salt and garam masala. Serve hot with rice, and a yogurt and cucumber salad.

BAKED AUBERGINE WITH COURGETTE

serves **4**

2 large aubergines
olive oil, for brushing
2 large courgettes, sliced
4 tomatoes, sliced
1 garlic clove, finely chopped
15 g/½ oz dry breadcrumbs
15 g/½ oz freshly grated vegetarian
   Parmesan-style cheese
salt and pepper
basil leaves, to garnish

A Mediterranean-inspired dish that combines the familiar vegetable mix of ratatouille in a crumb-topped bake. Fresh basil just adds the final flavour.

1. Cut the aubergines into fairly thin slices and brush with oil. Heat a large griddle pan or heavy-based frying pan over a high heat, then add the aubergines and cook in batches for 6–8 minutes, turning once, until soft and brown.

2. Layer the aubergines in the slow cooker with the courgettes, tomatoes and garlic, seasoning with salt and pepper between the layers.

3. Mix the breadcrumbs with the cheese and sprinkle over the vegetables. Cover and cook on low for 4 hours.

4. Transfer to warmed serving bowls, garnish with basil leaves and serve immediately.

TOFU WITH SPICY PEANUT SAUCE

serves **4**

675 g/1 lb 8 oz extra-firm tofu
2 tbsp vegetable oil
85 g/3 oz smooth peanut butter
3 tbsp low-sodium soy sauce
3 tbsp unseasoned rice vinegar
juice of 1 lime
2 tbsp soft light brown sugar
2 tsp toasted sesame oil
2 garlic cloves, finely chopped
1 tbsp finely chopped fresh ginger
2 jalapeño chillies, cored,
   deseeded and finely chopped
350 g/12 oz baby spinach leaves
chopped fresh coriander, to serve
steamed rice, to serve

Nutritious tofu gets a powerful punch of flavour from a combination of peanut butter, garlic, chillies and coriander.

1. Slice the tofu into 2.5-cm/1-inch thick slabs and pat very dry with kitchen paper, pressing to release any excess moisture. Cut into 2.5-cm/1-inch cubes.

2. Heat the vegetable oil in a large, non-stick frying pan over a medium–high heat. Add the tofu, in batches, if necessary, and cook on one side for about 3 minutes, until brown. Turn and cook on the other side for a further 3 minutes, until brown.

3. Meanwhile, put the peanut butter, soy sauce, vinegar, lime juice, sugar, sesame oil, garlic, ginger and chillies into the slow cooker and mix to combine.

4. Add the tofu to the slow cooker. Stir gently to coat, cover and cook on low for about 4 hours.

5. About 15 minutes before serving, place the spinach in the slow cooker on top of the cooked tofu mixture, cover and cook for about 15 minutes, until the spinach is wilted. Stir in the coriander and serve immediately with steamed rice.

MIXED BEAN CHILLI

serves **4 – 6**

115 g/4 oz dried red kidney beans,
    soaked overnight, drained and rinsed
115 g/4 oz dried black beans, soaked
    overnight, drained and rinsed
115 g/4 oz dried pinto beans, soaked
    overnight, drained and rinsed
2 tbsp corn oil
1 onion, chopped
1 garlic clove, finely chopped
1 fresh red chilli, deseeded and chopped
1 yellow pepper, deseeded and chopped
1 tsp ground cumin
1 tbsp chilli powder
1 litre/1¾ pints vegetable stock
1 tbsp sugar
salt and pepper
chopped fresh coriander, to garnish
crusty bread, to serve

Serve a warming bowl of this comfort food with baked potato wedges and an avocado, tomato and onion salad. If you eat dairy products, top with sour cream.

1. Place all the beans in a saucepan, cover with fresh cold water and bring to the boil. Boil rapidly for at least 10 minutes, then remove from the heat, drain and rinse again.

2. Heat the oil in a large, heavy-based saucepan. Add the onion, garlic, chilli and yellow pepper and cook over a medium heat, stirring occasionally, for 5 minutes. Stir in the cumin and chilli powder and cook, stirring, for 1–2 minutes. Add the drained beans and stock and bring to the boil. Boil vigorously for 15 minutes.

3. Transfer the mixture to the slow cooker, cover and cook on low for 10 hours, until the beans are tender.

4. Season to taste with salt and pepper, then ladle about one third into a bowl. Mash well with a potato masher, then return the mashed beans to the slow cooker and stir in the sugar. Transfer to warmed serving bowls and garnish with chopped coriander. Serve immediately with crusty bread.

STUFFED BUTTERNUT SQUASH

serves **4**

2 tbsp olive oil

1 shallot, diced

2 garlic cloves, finely chopped

250 g/9 oz chard, stems and thick centre ribs removed and leaves cut into wide ribbons

¾ tsp salt

1 tsp paprika

450 ml/16 fl oz vegetable stock

175 g/6 oz quinoa

425 g/15 oz canned cannellini beans, rinsed and drained

25 g/1 oz stoned Kalamata olives, diced

115 g/4 oz feta cheese, crumbled

2 tbsp finely chopped fresh mint leaves

2 butternut squash, halved and deseeded

To make the squash easier to cut, make a slit in the skin and heat in the microwave on high for 3–5 minutes.

1. Heat the oil in a large frying pan over a medium–high heat. Add the shallot and garlic and cook, stirring, for about 5 minutes, until soft. Add the chard and cook for about 3 minutes, until wilted. Add the salt and paprika and cook for a further 1 minute. Add the stock and quinoa and bring to the boil. Reduce the heat to low, cover and simmer for 15–20 minutes, until the quinoa is cooked through.

2. Stir in the beans, olives, half of the cheese and the mint.

3. Fill the slow cooker with water to a depth of 5 mm/¼ inch. Divide the quinoa mixture between the squash halves, then place them in the slow cooker, stuffed side up. Cover and cook on low for 6 hours.

4. Preheat the grill. Remove the squash halves from the slow cooker and top with the remaining cheese. Cook under the preheated grill for about 3 minutes, until the cheese is beginning to brown. Serve hot.

MACARONI CHEESE WITH TOASTED BREADCRUMBS

serves **4**

vegetable oil, for brushing
2 tbsp butter
2 tbsp plain flour
150 ml/5 fl oz vegetable stock
450 ml/16 fl oz evaporated milk
1½ tsp mustard powder
⅛–¼ tsp cayenne pepper
1 tsp salt
175 g/6 oz vegetarian Gruyère cheese,
　　grated
175 g/6 oz vegetarian fontina cheese,
　　grated
55 g/2 oz freshly grated vegetarian
　　Parmesan-style cheese
350 g/12 oz dried elbow macaroni
350 ml/12 fl oz water

Topping
2 thick slices French bread or
　　sourdough bread
2 tbsp butter

This classic comfort food dish is a breeze to make in the slow cooker. A toasted breadcrumb topping cooked on the hob adds a welcome crunch.

1. Line the slow cooker with foil and brush with a little oil.

2. Melt the butter in a large frying pan or saucepan over a medium–high heat. Whisk in the flour and cook for 1 minute. Reduce the heat to medium and slowly add the stock, evaporated milk, mustard, cayenne pepper and salt. Cook, stirring, for about 3–5 minutes, until thick. Add all the cheeses and whisk until melted. Add the macaroni and stir to mix well. Transfer to the slow cooker.

3. Add the water and stir to mix. Cover and cook on high for about 2 hours or on low for about 4 hours, until the macaroni is tender.

4. To make the topping, process the bread in a food processor to make crumbs. Melt the butter in a large frying pan over a medium heat until bubbling. Add the breadcrumbs and cook, stirring frequently, for about 5 minutes, until toasted and golden brown.

5. Serve hot, topped with the breadcrumbs.

WHITE BEAN STEW

serves **4**

2 tbsp olive oil
1 onion, diced
2 garlic cloves, finely chopped
2 carrots, diced
2 celery sticks, diced
175 g/6 oz canned tomato purée
1 tsp salt
½ tsp pepper
¼–½ tsp crushed dried red pepper flakes
1 bay leaf
225 ml/8 fl oz dry white wine
850 g/1 lb 14 oz canned cannellini beans,
    rinsed and drained
250 g/9 oz chard, kale or other winter
    green, stems and thick centre ribs
    removed, leaves cut into wide ribbons
225 ml/8 fl oz water
25 g/1 oz freshly grated vegetarian
    Parmesan-style cheese, to serve

A satisfying dish on its own, this rich and healthy stew is even better topped with a poached egg.

1. Heat the oil in a large frying pan over a medium–high heat. Add the onion and garlic and cook, stirring, for about 5 minutes, until soft. Add the carrots and celery and cook for a further few minutes. Stir in the tomato purée, salt, pepper, red pepper flakes and bay leaf, then add the wine.

2. Bring to the boil and cook, stirring and scraping up any sediment from the base of the pan, for about 5 minutes, until most of the liquid has evaporated. Transfer the mixture to the slow cooker.

3. Stir in the beans, chard and water. Cover and cook on high for 3 hours or on low for 6 hours. Serve hot, garnished with the cheese.

VEGETARIAN PAELLA

serves **6**

4 tbsp olive oil

1 Spanish onion, sliced

2 garlic cloves, finely chopped

1 litre/1¾ pints hot vegetable stock

large pinch of saffron threads,
   lightly crushed

1 yellow pepper, deseeded and sliced

1 red pepper, deseeded and sliced

1 large aubergine, diced

225 g/8 oz paella or risotto rice

450 g/1 lb tomatoes, peeled and chopped

115 g/4 oz chestnut mushrooms, sliced

115 g/4 oz French beans, halved

400 g/14 oz canned borlotti beans,
   drained and rinsed

salt and pepper

A delicious vegetarian version of the Spanish classic. If you include fish and seafood in your diet, you could add cooked prawns just before serving.

1. Heat the oil in a large frying pan. Add the onion and garlic and cook over a low heat, stirring occasionally, for 5 minutes, until softened. Put 3 tablespoons of the hot stock into a small bowl and stir in the saffron, then set aside to infuse.

2. Add the peppers and aubergine to the pan and cook, stirring occasionally, for 5 minutes. Add the rice and cook, stirring constantly, for 1 minute, until the grains are coated with oil and glistening. Pour in the remaining stock and add the tomatoes, mushrooms, French beans and borlotti beans. Stir in the saffron mixture and season to taste with salt and pepper.

3. Transfer the mixture to the slow cooker, cover and cook on low for 2½–3 hours, until the rice is tender and the stock has been absorbed. Transfer to warmed serving plates and serve immediately.

SPAGHETTI WITH LENTIL BOLOGNESE SAUCE

serves **4 – 6**

2 tbsp olive oil
1 onion, diced
2 garlic cloves, finely chopped
1 carrot, diced
2 celery sticks, diced
4 large mushrooms, diced
1 tbsp tomato purée
1 tsp salt
1 tsp crumbled dried oregano
1 bay leaf
400 g/14 oz canned chopped tomatoes,
   with juice
50 g/1¾ oz dried lentils
225 ml/8 fl oz water
450 g/1 lb dried spaghetti

Here, old-fashioned spag bol gets a healthy vegetarian makeover – which doesn't skimp on flavour.

1. Heat the oil in a large frying pan over a medium–high heat. Add the onion and garlic and cook, stirring, for about 5 minutes, until soft. Add the carrot, celery and mushrooms and continue to cook, stirring occasionally, for a further 5 minutes, or until the mushrooms are soft. Stir in the tomato purée, salt, oregano and bay leaf and cook, stirring, for a further 1 minute. Transfer the mixture to the slow cooker.

2. Stir in the tomatoes with their can juices, lentils and water. Cover and cook on high for 8 hours.

3. Just before serving, cook the spaghetti according to the packet directions. Serve the sauce hot over the spaghetti.

ASPARAGUS & SPINACH RISOTTO

serves **4**

2 tbsp olive oil

4 shallots, finely chopped

280 g/10 oz arborio rice

1 garlic clove, crushed

100 ml/3½ fl oz dry white wine

850 ml/1½ pints vegetable stock

200 g/7 oz asparagus spears

200 g/7 oz baby spinach leaves

40 g/1½ oz freshly grated vegetarian
    Parmesan-style cheese

salt and pepper

Cooking risotto this way removes the tedious stirring usually associated with the classic Italian dish. Arborio rice is used because it creates the right creaminess.

1. Heat the oil in a frying pan, add the shallots and fry over a medium heat, stirring, for 2–3 minutes. Add the rice and garlic and cook for a further 2 minutes, stirring. Add the wine and allow it to boil for 30 seconds.

2. Transfer the rice mixture to the slow cooker, add the stock and season to taste with salt and pepper. Cover and cook on high for 2 hours, or until most of the liquid is absorbed.

3. Cut the asparagus into 4-cm/1½-inch lengths. Stir into the rice, then spread the spinach over the top. Replace the lid and cook on high for a further 30 minutes, until the asparagus is just tender and the spinach is wilted.

4. Stir in the spinach with the cheese, then adjust the seasoning to taste and serve immediately in warmed bowls.

CHAPTER 5
DESSERTS & CAKES

CRÈME BRÛLÉE

serves **6**

1 vanilla pod
1 litre/1¾ pints double cream
6 egg yolks
100 g/3½ oz caster sugar
85 g/3 oz soft light brown sugar

Using this method to cook the custard gently will ensure your crème brûlée doesn't curdle.

1. Using a sharp knife, split the vanilla pod in half lengthways, scrape the seeds into a saucepan and add the pod. Pour in the cream and bring just to the boil, stirring constantly. Remove from the heat, cover and leave to infuse for 20 minutes.

2. Whisk together the egg yolks and caster sugar in a bowl until thoroughly mixed. Remove and discard the vanilla pod from the pan, then whisk the cream into the egg yolk mixture. Strain the mixture into a large jug.

3. Divide the mixture among six ramekins and cover with foil. Stand the ramekins on a trivet in the slow cooker and pour in enough boiling water to come about halfway up the sides of the ramekins. Cover and cook on low for 3–3½ hours, until just set. Remove the slow cooker insert from the base and leave to cool completely, then remove the ramekins and chill in the refrigerator for at least 4 hours.

4. Preheat the grill to high. Sprinkle the brown sugar evenly over the surface of each dessert, then cook under the preheated grill for 30–60 seconds, until the sugar has melted and caramelized. Alternatively, you can use a cook's blowtorch. Return the ramekins to the refrigerator and chill for a further hour before serving.

DOUBLE CHOCOLATE COOKIES

makes about **18**

125 g/4½ oz plain flour
85 g/3 oz cocoa powder
½ tsp baking powder
¼ tsp salt
115 g/4 oz unsalted butter, softened,
    plus extra for greasing
100 g/3½ oz sugar
1 large egg
1 tsp vanilla extract
25 g/1 oz plain chocolate chips

Although they look more like brownies than traditional round cookies, these luxurious treats will win plenty of fans. The larger your slow cooker, the thinner these cookies will be. For best results, use a 4–4.5-litre/ 7–8-pint round or oval slow cooker.

1. Generously grease the inside of the slow cooker with butter.

2. Put the flour, cocoa powder, baking powder and salt into a medium-sized bowl and mix to combine. Put the butter and sugar into a large bowl and cream together. Add the egg and vanilla extract and beat well together. Gradually beat in the flour mixture until well incorporated. Stir in the chocolate chips.

3. Using a rubber spatula, scrape the batter into the prepared slow cooker and smooth the top. Cover and cook on low for 2½ hours. Set the lid slightly ajar and continue to cook on low for a further 30 minutes.

4. Leaving the cookie on the ceramic insert, remove it from the slow cooker and transfer to a wire rack to cool for 30 minutes. Turn the cookie out onto the rack and leave to cool for a further 30 minutes before slicing it into 5-cm/2-inch pieces. Serve at room temperature.

LEMON SPONGE

serves **4**

140 g/5 oz caster sugar
3 eggs, separated
300 ml/10 fl oz milk
3 tbsp self-raising flour, sifted
150 ml/5 fl oz lemon juice
icing sugar, for dusting

This recipe will amaze you as the cooked mixture separates to create a light sponge sitting on top of a delicious lemony sauce.

1. Using an electric mixer, beat the caster sugar with the egg yolks in a bowl. Gradually beat in the milk, followed by the flour and the lemon juice.

2. Whisk the egg whites in a separate grease-free bowl until stiff. Fold half the whites into the yolk mixture using a plastic spatula in a figure-of-eight movement, then fold in the remainder. Try not to knock out the air.

3. Pour the mixture into a heatproof dish and cover with foil. Stand the dish on a trivet in the slow cooker and pour in enough boiling water to come about one third of the way up the side of the dish. Cover and cook on high for 2½ hours, until the mixture has set and the sauce and sponge have separated.

4. Carefully remove the dish from the slow cooker and discard the foil. Transfer to warmed bowls, lightly dust with icing sugar and serve immediately.

BROWN SUGAR APPLE CAKE

serves **6 – 8**

185 g/6½ oz self-raising flour
½ tsp ground cinnamon
½ tsp bicarbonate of soda
¼ tsp salt
115 g/4 oz unsalted butter, softened,
   plus extra for greasing
225 g/8 oz soft light brown sugar
100 g/3½ oz granulated sugar
2 large eggs, lightly beaten
1 tsp vanilla extract
1 large apple, peeled, cored and diced
whipped cream, to serve (optional)

This moist apple-cinnamon cake is delicious for dessert, or as a sweet brunch treat. This recipe works best with a 3.8-litre/7-pint slow cooker.

1. Grease the inside of the slow cooker with butter.

2. Put the flour, cinnamon, bicarbonate of soda and salt into a medium-sized bowl and mix to combine. Put the butter, brown sugar and granulated sugar into a large bowl and cream together with an electric mixer.

3. Add the eggs and vanilla extract and beat on high for about 3 minutes. Gradually add the flour mixture to the sugar mixture, beating until fully incorporated. Stir in the apple.

4. Pour the mixture into the prepared slow cooker. Cover and cook on low for 2½–3 hours, until a skewer inserted into the centre of the cake comes out clean.

5. Leaving the cake on the ceramic insert, remove it from the slow cooker and transfer to a wire rack to cool for at least 60 minutes. Run a thin knife around the outside of the cake to release it from the sides of the insert, then turn it out onto a serving platter.

6. To serve, slice into wedges and top with a dollop of whipped cream, if using.

STRAWBERRY CHEESECAKE

serves **6 – 8**

85 g/3 oz unsalted butter, melted
140 g/5 oz digestive biscuits, crushed
300 g/10½ oz strawberries, hulled
600 g/1 lb 5 oz full fat soft cheese
225 g/8 oz caster sugar
2 large eggs, beaten
2 tbsp cornflour
finely grated rind and juice of 1 lemon

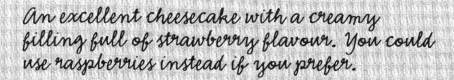

An excellent cheesecake with a creamy filling full of strawberry flavour. You could use raspberries instead if you prefer.

1. Stir the butter into the crushed biscuits and press into the base of a 20-cm/8-inch round springform tin, or a tin that fits into your slow cooker.

2. Purée or mash half the strawberries and whisk together with the cheese, sugar, eggs, cornflour, lemon rind and juice until smooth.

3. Tip the mixture into the tin and place in the slow cooker. Cover and cook on high for about 2 hours or until almost set.

4. Turn off the slow cooker and leave the cheesecake in the cooker for 2 hours. Remove and cool completely, then carefully turn out of the tin.

5. Decorate with the remaining sliced strawberries and serve.

CARROT CAKE

serves **8 – 10**

125 g/4½ oz plain flour
1 tsp bicarbonate of soda
¼ tsp salt
½ tsp ground cinnamon
pinch of ground nutmeg
2 large eggs
100 g/3½ oz granulated sugar
55 g/2 oz soft light brown sugar
4 tbsp vegetable oil, plus extra
   for greasing
150 ml/5 fl oz buttermilk
1 tsp vanilla extract
450 g/1 lb carrots, grated
60 g/2¾ oz desiccated coconut
35 g/1¼ oz sultanas (optional)
whipped cream, to serve

A 3.8-litre / 7-pint round or oval slow cooker is perfect for this moist and delicious cake. If using a larger or smaller slow cooker, the cooking time may need to be adjusted. Check whether the cake is ready every 15 minutes, after 1½ hours' cooking.

1. Grease the inside of the slow cooker with oil.

2. Put the flour, bicarbonate of soda, salt, cinnamon and nutmeg into a small bowl and mix to combine. Put the eggs, granulated sugar and brown sugar into a medium-sized bowl and whisk together until well combined. Add the oil, buttermilk and vanilla extract and stir to combine. Add the egg mixture to the flour mixture and mix well. Fold in the carrots and coconut, and the sultanas, if using.

3. Pour the mixture into the prepared slow cooker. Place several sheets of kitchen paper on top of the slow cooker, then put the lid on top to secure the kitchen paper in place above the cake mixture. Cook on low for about 2 hours, until a skewer inserted into the centre of the cake comes out clean.

4. Leaving the cake in the ceramic insert, remove it from the slow cooker and transfer to a wire rack to cool for at least 30 minutes. Cut the cake into wedges and serve it directly from the insert. Serve warm or at room temperature with a dollop of whipped cream.

Desserts & Cakes 192

RICE PUDDING

serves **4**

140 g/5 oz short-grain rice
1 litre/1¾ pints milk
115 g/4 oz sugar
1 tsp vanilla extract
ground cinnamon, for dusting

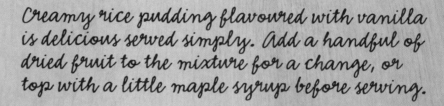

Creamy rice pudding flavoured with vanilla is delicious served simply. Add a handful of dried fruit to the mixture for a change, or top with a little maple syrup before serving.

1. Rinse the rice well under cold running water and drain thoroughly. Pour the milk into a large heavy-based saucepan, add the sugar and bring to the boil, stirring constantly. Sprinkle in the rice, stir well and simmer gently for 10–15 minutes. Transfer the mixture to a heatproof dish and cover with foil.

2. Stand the dish on a trivet in the slow cooker and pour in enough boiling water to come about one third of the way up the side of the dish. Cover and cook on high for 2 hours.

3. Remove the dish from the slow cooker and discard the foil. Stir the vanilla extract into the rice, then spoon it into warmed bowls. Lightly dust with cinnamon and serve immediately.

MINI PUMPKIN CHEESECAKES WITH GINGERNUT CRUST

serves **4**

Base
115 g/4 oz gingernut biscuits, crushed
2 tbsp soft light brown sugar
pinch of salt
3 tbsp unsalted butter, melted

Filling
1 tbsp flour
¼ tsp ground cinnamon
pinch of grated nutmeg
pinch of salt
2 large eggs
100 g/3½ oz soft light brown sugar
115 g/4 oz cream cheese
200 g/7 oz pumpkin purée
2 tbsp double cream
2 tsp vanilla extract
1 tbsp whisky
icing sugar, for dusting

Spicy gingernuts provide a crunchy base for a rich, pumpkin-flavoured cheesecake filling.

1. To make the base, preheat the oven to 190°C/375°F/ Gas Mark 5. Put the crushed gingernuts, sugar and salt into a food processor and pulse several times. Add the butter and pulse until well combined. Press the mixture into the bases and about three quarters of the way up the sides of four 225-ml/8-fl oz ramekins. Place the ramekins on a baking tray and bake in the preheated oven for 10 minutes. Leave to cool.

2. To make the filling, put the flour, cinnamon, nutmeg and salt into a large bowl and whisk together. Whisk in the eggs, sugar, cream cheese, pumpkin purée, cream, vanilla extract and whisky.

3. Spoon the filling into the ramekins and place the ramekins in the slow cooker. Carefully add boiling water to a depth of 4 cm/1½ inches. Cover and cook on high for about 2 hours, until the filling is set. Turn off the slow cooker and leave the ramekins inside for a further 1 hour, then remove them from the slow cooker and chill in the refrigerator for at least 2 hours. Dust with icing sugar before serving.

CHOCOLATE POTS

serves **6**

300 ml/10 fl oz single cream
300 ml/10 fl oz milk
225 g/8 oz plain chocolate,
    broken into small pieces
1 large egg
4 egg yolks
4 tbsp caster sugar
150 ml/5 fl oz double cream
chocolate curls, to decorate

*A favourite dessert for chocolate lovers.
Make this recipe the day before to allow the
chocolate to set firmly and become gooey.*

1. Pour the single cream and milk into a saucepan and add the chocolate. Set the pan over a very low heat and stir until the chocolate has melted and the mixture is smooth. Remove from the heat and leave to cool for 10 minutes.

2. Beat together the egg, egg yolks and sugar in a bowl until combined. Gradually stir in the chocolate mixture until thoroughly blended, then strain into a jug.

3. Divide the mixture among six ramekins and cover with foil. Stand the ramekins on a trivet in the slow cooker and pour in enough boiling water to come about halfway up the sides of the ramekins. Cover and cook on low for 3–3½ hours, until just set. Remove the slow cooker insert and leave to cool completely, then remove the ramekins and chill in the refrigerator for at least 4 hours.

4. Whip the double cream in a bowl until it holds soft peaks. Top each chocolate pot with a little of the whipped cream and decorate with chocolate curls. Serve immediately.

STUFFED APPLES

serves **4**

4 large cooking apples
175 g/6 oz soft light brown sugar
25 g/1 oz rolled oats
1 tsp ground cinnamon
4 tbsp butter, cut into small pieces
2 tbsp sultanas
25 g/1 oz pecan nuts or walnuts,
   roughly chopped
whipped cream, to serve

This simple dessert is a lot healthier than apple pie, but just as delicious.

1. Use a paring knife to cut the stem end out of each apple, then scoop out the core with a melon baller or teaspoon, leaving the base of the apple intact.

2. To make the filling, put the sugar, oats, cinnamon and butter into a bowl and mix together with a fork. Add the sultanas and nuts and toss to mix well. Stuff the mixture into the apples, dividing it evenly.

3. Pour 125 ml/4 fl oz of water into the slow cooker, then carefully add the apples, standing them up in the base of the slow cooker. Cover and cook on high for about 1½ hours or on low for 3 hours. Serve the apples hot, topped with whipped cream.

POACHED PEACHES IN MARSALA

serves **4 – 6**

150 ml/5 fl oz Marsala
175 ml/6 fl oz water
4 tbsp caster sugar
1 vanilla pod, split lengthways
6 peaches, cut into wedges and stoned
2 tsp cornflour
crème fraîche or Greek yogurt, to serve

Marsala is a fortified wine from Sicily, it is similar to port. Use in dessert recipes such as tiramisu or with fruit such as peaches and nectarines.

1. Pour the Marsala and 150 ml/5 fl oz of the water into a saucepan and add the sugar and vanilla pod. Set the pan over a low heat and stir until the sugar has dissolved, then bring to the boil without stirring. Remove from the heat.

2. Put the peaches into the slow cooker and pour the syrup over them. Cover and cook on high for 1–1½ hours, until the fruit is tender.

3. Using a slotted spoon, gently transfer the peaches to a serving dish. Remove the vanilla pod from the slow cooker and scrape the seeds into the syrup with the point of a knife. Discard the pod. Stir the cornflour to a paste with the remaining water in a small bowl, then stir into the syrup. Re-cover and cook on high for 15 minutes, stirring occasionally.

4. Spoon the syrup over the fruit and leave to cool slightly. Serve warm or chill in the refrigerator for 2 hours before serving with crème fraîche or yogurt.

CARAMELIZED BANANA UPSIDE-DOWN CAKE

serves **6 – 8**

175 g/6 oz plain flour
55 g/2 oz soft light brown sugar
150 g/5½ oz granulated sugar
¾ tsp bicarbonate of soda
½ tsp baking powder
½ tsp salt
3 tbsp unsalted butter
2 ripe bananas
125 ml/4 fl oz buttermilk
1 tsp vanilla extract
2 eggs

Caramelized banana
5 tbsp unsalted butter
175 g/6 oz soft light brown sugar
pinch of salt
2 small ripe bananas, sliced

This retro-hip 1950s throwback is easy to make, fun to serve, and delicious to eat.

1. To make the caramelized banana, put the butter into an 18 cm/ 7 inch soufflé dish and place it in the microwave on high for about 1 minute, until melted. Tilt the dish to coat the sides and base with the butter, then stir in the sugar and the salt. Spread the mixture evenly over the base of the dish. Add the sliced bananas on top, ideally in a single layer, or overlapping slightly if necessary.

2. Put the flour, brown sugar, granulated sugar, bicarbonate of soda, baking powder and salt into a medium-sized bowl and mix to combine. Put the butter into a large bowl and place it in the microwave on high for about 1 minute, until melted. Add the bananas and mash them into the butter. Whisk in the buttermilk, vanilla extract and eggs. Add the flour mixture to the butter mixture and whisk until thoroughly combined.

3. Pour the cake mixture over the sliced bananas in the soufflé dish and place in the slow cooker on a trivet. Cover and cook on low for 2 hours, until cooked through. Turn off the cooker and leave the cake in it for a further 30 minutes.

4. Leave the soufflé dish in the ceramic insert, remove them both from the slow cooker and transfer to a wire rack to cool for 15 minutes. Run a thin knife around the edge of the cake to release it from the sides of the dish, then turn it out onto a serving platter. Slice into wedges and serve.

ITALIAN BREAD PUDDING

serves **6**

unsalted butter, for greasing
6 slices panettone
3 tbsp Marsala
300 ml/10 fl oz milk
300 ml/10 fl oz single cream
100 g/3½ oz caster sugar
grated rind of ½ lemon
pinch of ground cinnamon
3 large eggs, lightly beaten

A great variation on traditional bread and butter pudding. Panettone is an Italian fruit loaf available mainly at Christmas, but you can use any sweet fruit bread or brioche.

1. Grease a 1-litre/1¾-pint pudding basin with butter. Place the panettone on a deep plate and sprinkle with the Marsala.

2. Pour the milk and cream into a pan and add the sugar, lemon rind and cinnamon. Gradually bring to the boil over a low heat, stirring until the sugar has dissolved. Remove the pan from the heat and leave to cool slightly, then pour the mixture onto the eggs, beating constantly.

3. Place the panettone in the prepared basin, pour in the egg mixture and cover with foil. Stand the basin on a trivet in the slow cooker and pour in enough boiling water to come about one third of the way up the side of the basin. Cover and cook on high for 2½ hours, until set.

4. Carefully remove the basin from the slow cooker and discard the foil. Leave to cool, then chill in the refrigerator until required. Run a knife around the inside of the basin, then turn out onto a serving dish. Serve immediately.

BUTTERSCOTCH PUDDINGS

serves **6**

2 tbsp unsalted butter
275 g/9¾ oz soft dark brown sugar
½ tsp salt
300 ml/10 fl oz double cream
175 ml/6 fl oz milk
4 egg yolks, lightly beaten
2 tsp vanilla extract
2 tsp whisky
whipped cream, to serve

These rich and creamy butterscotch puddings are a cinch to make in the slow cooker.

1. Fill the slow cooker with water to a depth of about 4 cm/1½ inches.

2. Melt the butter in a large saucepan over a medium heat. Add the sugar and salt and stir to mix well. Add the cream and milk and heat over a medium heat, until hot but not boiling.

3. Place the egg yolks in a medium-sized mixing bowl. Add the sugar and milk mixture in a very thin stream, whisking constantly. Whisk in the vanilla extract and whisky. Ladle the mixture into six 125-ml/4-fl oz ramekins.

4. Carefully place the ramekins in the slow cooker, taking care not to slosh any of the water into them. Cover the slow cooker and cook on low for about 2 hours, or until the puddings are set.

5. Remove the ramekins from the slow cooker and transfer to a wire rack to cool for about 15 minutes, then cover with clingfilm, place in the refrigerator and chill for at least 2 hours before serving. Serve chilled, topped with a dollop of whipped cream.

CHOCOLATE CAKE

serves **8**

375 g/13 oz plain chocolate,
   broken into pieces
175 g/6 oz unsalted butter,
   plus extra for greasing
175 g/6 oz light muscovado sugar
4 eggs
2 tsp vanilla extract
150 g/5½ oz self-raising flour
55 g/2 oz ground almonds
125 ml/4 fl oz double cream
icing sugar, for dusting

Everyone loves chocolate cake and this recipe will become a favourite. For a special occasion sprinkle fresh raspberries on top of the filling.

1. Place a trivet or a ring of crumpled foil in the base of the slow cooker. Grease and base-line a 20-cm/8-inch diameter, deep cake tin, or a tin that fits into your slow cooker.

2. Melt 250 g/9 oz chocolate in a bowl over a pan of simmering water. Remove from the heat and cool slightly.

3. Beat the butter and sugar in a large bowl until pale and fluffy. Gradually beat in the eggs. Stir in the melted chocolate and 1 teaspoon of vanilla extract. Fold in the flour and almonds evenly.

4. Spoon the mixture into the tin, spreading evenly. Place in the slow cooker, cover and cook on high for 2½ hours or until risen and springy to the touch.

5. Remove from the slow cooker and leave the cake in the tin for 10 minutes. Turn out and cool on a wire rack.

6. Place the remaining chocolate and vanilla extract with the cream in a pan and heat gently, stirring, until melted. Cool until thick enough to spread. Split the cake into two layers and sandwich together with the filling. Dust with icing sugar to serve.

APPLE CRUMBLE

serves **4 – 6**

100 g/3½ oz sugar

1 tbsp cornflour

1 tsp ground cinnamon

¼ tsp ground nutmeg

6 large cooking apples, peeled,
    cored and chopped

2 tbsp lemon juice

vanilla ice cream, to serve (optional)

Topping

60 g/2¼ oz plain flour

75 g/2¾ oz soft light brown sugar

3 tbsp granulated sugar

pinch of salt

3 tbsp unsalted butter,
    cut into small pieces

60 g/2¼ oz rolled oats

85 g/3 oz pecan nuts or walnuts,
    roughly chopped

This simple dessert will fill your house with the sweet smell of autumn, and it's the perfect way to end a meal on a chilly evening.

1. Put the sugar, cornflour, cinnamon and nutmeg into the slow cooker and stir to combine. Add the apples and lemon juice and toss to coat well.

2. To make the topping, put the flour, brown sugar, granulated sugar and salt into a large mixing bowl and mix to combine. Using two knives, cut the butter into the flour mixture until it resembles coarse crumbs. Add the oats and nuts and toss until well combined.

3. Sprinkle the topping evenly over the apple mixture, cover and cook on high for about 2 hours or on low for about 4 hours, until the apples are soft. Set the lid ajar and cook for a further 1 hour, or until the topping is crisp. Serve warm, topped with vanilla ice cream, if using.

BLUSHING PEARS

serves **6**

6 small ripe pears
225 ml/8 fl oz ruby port
200 g/7 oz caster sugar
1 tsp finely chopped crystallized ginger
2 tbsp lemon juice
whipped cream or Greek yogurt, to serve

A port-flavoured syrup tints the pears a delicate pink colour as they cook. Madeira could be used instead of port and the ginger could be replaced with a cinnamon stick.

1. Peel the pears, cut them in half lengthways and scoop out the cores. Place them in the slow cooker.

2. Combine the port, sugar, ginger and lemon juice in a jug and pour the mixture over the pears. Cover and cook on low for 4 hours, until the pears are tender.

3. Leave the pears to cool in the slow cooker, then carefully transfer to a bowl and chill in the refrigerator until required.

4. To serve, cut each pear half into about six slices lengthways, leaving the fruit intact at the stalk end. Carefully lift the pear halves onto serving plates and press gently to fan out the slices. Spoon the cooking juices over the pears and serve immediately with cream.

GINGER CAKE

serves **8 – 10**

115 g/4 oz unsalted butter, melted,
    plus extra for greasing
85 g/3 oz soft light brown sugar
150 ml/5 fl oz golden syrup
1 tsp vanilla extract
175 g/6 oz plain flour
2 tsp ground ginger
1½ tsp bicarbonate of soda
pinch of salt
2 large eggs, lightly beaten
125 ml/4 fl oz milk
whipped cream, to serve

This moist, spicy ginger cake is even better the day after it is made. After cooling, cover loosely with foil and store at room temperature.

1. Grease the base and sides of an 18-cm/7-inch soufflé dish. Fill the slow cooker with hot (not boiling) water to a depth of about 2.5 cm/1 inch.

2. Put the butter, sugar, golden syrup and vanilla extract into a medium-sized bowl and stir to mix well. Put the flour, ginger, bicarbonate of soda, and salt into a large mixing bowl and stir to combine. Stir the butter mixture into the flour mixture with a wooden spoon and mix together until well combined. Add the eggs and milk and continue to mix until smooth.

3. Pour the mixture into the prepared soufflé dish and carefully place it in the slow cooker. Cover and cook on low for about 3 hours, until a skewer inserted into the centre of the cake comes out clean. Leave the soufflé dish in the ceramic insert, remove them both from the slow cooker and transfer to a wire rack to cool for at least 30 minutes, then remove the soufflé dish from the insert and leave to cool for a further 30 minutes.

4. To serve, slice the cake into wedges and top with a dollop of whipped cream.

ALMOND CHARLOTTE

serves **4**

unsalted butter, for greasing
10–12 sponge fingers
300 ml/10 fl oz milk
2 eggs
2 tbsp caster sugar
55 g/2 oz blanched almonds, chopped
4–5 drops of almond extract

Sherry sauce
1 tbsp caster sugar
3 egg yolks
150 ml/5 fl oz cream sherry

1. Grease a 600-ml/1-pint pudding basin with butter. Line the basin with the sponge fingers, cutting them to fit and placing them cut-ends down and sugar-coated sides outwards. Cover the base of the basin with some of the offcuts.

2. Pour the milk into a saucepan and bring just to the boil, then remove from the heat. Beat together the eggs and sugar in a heatproof bowl until combined, then stir in the milk. Stir in the almonds and almond extract.

3. Carefully pour the mixture into the prepared basin, making sure that the sponge fingers stay in place, and cover with foil. Stand the basin on a trivet in the slow cooker and pour in enough boiling water to come about halfway up the side of the dish. Cover and cook on high for 3–3½ hours, until set.

4. Shortly before serving, make the sherry sauce. Put the sugar, egg yolks and sherry into a heatproof bowl. Set the bowl over a pan of simmering water, without allowing the bottom of the bowl to touch the surface of the water. Whisk well until the mixture thickens, but do not allow it to boil. Remove from the heat.

5. Carefully remove the basin from the slow cooker and discard the foil. Leave to stand for 2–3 minutes, then turn out onto a warmed serving plate. Pour the sherry sauce around it and serve immediately.

CHOCOLATE FONDUE

serves **4 – 6**

butter, for greasing
225 ml/8 fl oz double cream
350 g/12 oz plain chocolate,
   chopped into small pieces
1 tsp vanilla extract

To serve
diced fruit (bananas, strawberries,
   apples, pears)
marshmallows
cookies or pieces of cake

This easy-to-make, yet decadent dessert is a fun way to end a dinner party.

1. Grease the inside of the slow cooker with butter.

2. Put the cream and chocolate into the slow cooker and stir to combine. Cover and cook on low, stirring occasionally, for 45–60 minutes, until the chocolate is completely melted. Stir in the vanilla extract.

3. Leave the mixture in the slow cooker or transfer to a fondue pot with a burner and serve immediately, with platters of diced fruit, marshmallows and cookies for dipping.